A DRAUGHT OF CONTENTMENT

A DRAUGHT
OF CONTENTMENT

*The Story of the
Courage Group*

John Pudney

NEW ENGLISH LIBRARY

TIMES MIRROR

First Published 1971 by New English Library, Barnards Inn,
Holborn, London E.C.1

450 00994 7

Printed and bound in Great Britain by
C. Tinling & Co. Ltd.
London and Prescot

CONTENTS

INTRODUCTION

The brewing industry is unique in its involvement with the nation. There are other industries making consumer goods such as clothing or grocery which are vertically integrated and have their retail shops; but brewing has as its main retail outlet some 75,000 pubs and bars, all different, all in some degree social centres and all characteristic of the British way of life.

A sense of continuity and tradition pervades the industry for British Beer and the British Pub have become cherished national symbols. Yet there has to be constant production serving needs and appetites which are never static: and throughout the years brewers, though traditionalists, have never been slow to adapt their resources and their policies to changing times. This was one of the first industries to take advantage of steam power. During the nineteen sixties the Courage Group alone spent £10m on production plant. But about 70% of the total capital in brewing lies in retail properties and something like £24,000,000 is spent by the industry annually on upkeep, improvement and construction of pubs and hotels.

More than any other industry brewing is involved with social legislation. Since the first introduction of licensing in Britain in 1552, there has been a massive structure of law regulating both the manufacture and distribution of beer, accompanied by complex systems of taxation. From a localised activity, from the cottage or farmhouse brewery in the country or the small family backstreet brewhouse in the towns, the industry grew with improved techniques and, above all, with the revolution in transport, into larger units. During the four hundred years since the first licensing, the progress of the industry has been marked

1

by mergers and amalgamations. The history of the Courage Group typically reflects this.

It also serves as an outstanding example of the potent family continuity which exists in brewing. Names which come into the story during the eighteenth century are still present, and significant, in the sixties of this century.

Since its formation in 1956, the Courage Group has emerged as one of the most potent forces in an industry which is as progressive and competitive as it has ever been. The stories of the five main components which form the Group have been told individually from material gathered in Southwark, Bermondsey, Reading, Bristol and Tadcaster and from the families who have been connected with some part of the enterprise for many generations.

COURAGE

1

It was what we would now call a shrewd diversification.

John Courage in 1787 was in the prime of life and in the course of eight years he had consolidated his position in London. He had come from Aberdeen as a younger son of a French Huguenot family exiled and settled in Scotland a century before. He had prospered in the flourishing maritime trade of the Thames tideway, acting as agent for Scottish interests, the Carron ships which plied from Glasgow Wharf on the north bank down stream from the Tower. From that base he cast his eyes across the busy river to the Southwark foreshore with its frieze of masts, rigging and furled sails and decided to diversify his interests by going into beer.

So the name of Courage was associated with brewing, with London, and with Southwark where in the fourteenth century Geoffrey Chaucer had celebrated the ale and primed his Canterbury pilgrimage on it. The association has had a triumphant continuity. There is still a Courage, John's direct descendant at the head of the business, and the punning slogan Take Courage has a national familiarity, its message often being taken as a moral exhortation by twentieth century pilgrims.

When John Courage settled for the purchase of a brew house at Horselydown across the river he was investing his acumen and money in a staple industry at an opportune time. The American Colonies had been lost for more than a decade, King George III was approaching his first bout of madness, yet Macaulay wrote that "The eight years which followed the General Elections of 1784 were as tranquil and prosperous as any eight years in the whole history of England."

In that pre-Industrial Revolution society, brewing was becoming one of the nation's foremost industries. The population was steadily increasing and the average household regarded ale and beer as a necessity, a staple item of diet for men, women and children upon which more money was spent than on any other commodity. Sidney and Beatrice Webb estimated that 100,000 ale-houses were serving a population of some eight million. More specific figures for production have survived. In the year that John Courage entered the business, Common Brewers and Brewing Victuallers produced over 14,350,000 barrels. This figure did not include the output of home and private brewers, whose activities in any case were beginning to diminish. The tendency was for brewing to develop in the hands of professionals from a mystery to an industry aware of scientific methods and capable of facing the problems of distribution.

John Courage may well have studied an influential work, *Philosophical Principles of the Science of Brewing* by John Richardson, published three years before he made his move. In this, the introduction of the thermometer "general as it is now becoming" and the saccharometer were taken for granted as scientific developments of that century. In more general terms Richardson also noticed changes in management: "The humble origin of the brewing business has long entailed a general concurrent opinion that its professors need neither genius nor education; and in conformity to that opinion, has this profession, more perhaps, than any other of the like national importance, been disgraced by sinking into the hands of the most ignorant and illiterate. ... It is, however, a happiness that the extensive connexions of modern times have induced men of fortune, education and liberality, in this country at least to adopt the profession, and render it respectable."

For a man of John Courage's generation, in the seventeen eighties there could have been little doubt about the respectability of the expanding profession. It had been socially acceptable for more than a hundred years, particularly in Southwark, as Peter Mathias noted: "In so far as business wealth became reflected in social position, this generation of the most important London brewers at the end of the seventeenth century shows a heightened status. Byde, whose ale Pepys thought it worth travelling out to Mile End to drink, was an Alderman of the City. George Meggott, Charles Cox, John Friend, John Lade, John Parsons and Felix Feast eventually became knights. A brewer's daughter married a peer. Several brewers were already Members of Parliament – in particular Southwark, a borough which had brewing as its major industry, was for long thus represented. There can be no more revealing evidence than this of the importance of the brewing industry in the locality – a prominence dating directly back to the settlement of German and Dutch beer brewers. Where indirect evidence must be relied on, parliamentary representation becomes as good a guide as any to social position and economic strength."

While family continuity such as that initiated by John Courage is one of the most remarkable features of the brewing industry – particularly strong in the Courage Group where there are not only Courages but Barclays and Simonds actively engaged in the business – there have always been times when new men, not brewers born and bred, entered the trade from outside. This intake of new blood to start a dynasty is traditional. It was explained by R. Campbell as early as 1747 in his *General Description of all Trades:* "The Brewer in London, as far as I can learn, seldom takes Apprentices; his work is carried on by Labourers who have acquired their Knowledge by Experience, and those who intend to set up Business have either been acquainted with it, by being Son or Relation to some Man in the Trade, or take their chance by depending on the Skill and Honesty of the Clerks and Servants. (Most new blood, in these circumstances, entered existing concerns) . . . in Proportion to what cash they can advance, which is the most common way of their coming first into trade, for to erect a Common Brewhouse and lay in Stock answerable, will sink many Thousands before they see any Returns."

John Courage's venture into diversification was in fact well timed and in keeping with his times. His choice of Horselydown for his venture was shrewd, so shrewd that the business to which he gave his name has never had to move. At that time there were plenty of small brewing concerns on the north bank of the Thames within the city boundaries close enough to the Carron and Continental Wharf (give it its present name) from which he conducted his shipping business. But Southwark brewing was already renowned and he wisely chose the south bank of the river for his investment. The ales of Southwark had long since been celebrated, particularly by Chaucer whose Canterbury pilgrims were well primed with the local brew before setting out for Canterbury. The cook's apprentice 'loved best the taverne than the schoppe'. The miller admits to being 'dronke' before setting out on his pilgrimage, and makes excuses for his condition 'wyte it the ale of Southwark I you preye'. Chaucer wrote *The Canterbury Tales* about 1387 and they were first printed by Caxton in 1475. The brewing of Southwark had therefore received a literary tribute some four hundred years before John Courage turned his attention to Horselydown.

His initial investment amounted to £616.13.11d. The money was paid by cheque dated December 20th 1787 which, in accordance with the custom of the time, does not bear the name of the payee. An invoice dated the year 1765 rendering an account for 45 firkins of beer at 2/6d each still exists and indicates that John and Hagger Allis of Horfly Down Old Stairs were the vendors, and probably these were the people who sold their interest to John Courage. A little more than a year later on January 4th 1789, there was the first entry in the brewing book stating that John Courage from Aberdeen had brewed 51 barrels of beer at The Anchor Brewhouse, Horselydown. No doubt his maritime connections inspired him to give this name to the new enterprise. There is no trace of its use before his takeover.

The 51 barrels of beer were a very modest start to what was to become a rapidly expanding enterprise. There were only ten years between his entry into the business and his death; but during that time his priorities changed. He became first a brewer and second a shipping man, and his portrait in oils which still hangs in the Board Room was captioned: "Picture of Mr. Courage, Brewer of Shad Thames, Agent for Carron Ships at Glasgow Wharf . . .". It was said to have been the excitement of a parliamentary election rather than the anxieties of business which caused his sudden death in the prime of life – as his portrait shows – in 1793.

In investing in this enterprise at Horselydown, Courage was not only buying his way into a local industry with deep and strong roots but he was also taking possession of property already established historically. There have been many spellings of the name which still appears in London Street Directories as Horselydown Lane, S.E.1. A map of 1544 has it as Horseye Downe. All variations agree at least in its literal meaning as an open space for pasturing the horses and cattle of the people of Southwark and Bermondsey. By the time Courage had moved in the whole area was built over. The eighteenth century had already industrialised it but then, as now, historical associations were kept alive in the place names. The narrow street called Shad Thames still bounds The Anchor Brewery. Its derivation has sometimes been ascribed to the shad fish which were plentiful in the earlier unpolluted Thames. But the more likely logical derivation is from the corruption, in popular speech, of "St. John at Thames", for the Knights of St. John of Jerusalem had been established in Horselydown for many centuries. It was in fact the site of the old "Knight's Hous" lying between the open space of Horseye Downe and the river which John Courage acquired. The property of the Knights Hospitallers, referred to as the Liberty of St. John of Jerusalem in the reign of Edward I consisted of three water-mills, three acres of land, one acre of meadow and twenty acres of pasture. In a survey of their estates in 1338 it was stated that: ". . . there are in Sutwerck two water-mills, one separate pasture, and three small pieces of meadow; and that the whole were demised to Hawise de Swal-clive, for the term of her life . . ."

9

In 1505 "Sir Thomas Docwra, Prior of the Hospital of St. John of Jerusalem in England, and his brethren, knights of the same hospital, demised to Ralph Bothomley of Horsadowne, yeoman, their water myln called, St. John's Myln, situate at Horsadowne in the county of Surrey, with all the meadows and pastures, housings and appurtenances, thereunto belonging, for the term of forty years, from St. John's Day then last, at the yearly rent of £8."

The knights continued to hold some part of their land until the dissolution of the monastries by Henry VIII, but their presence at Horselydown was overshadowed by that of Sir John Fastolfe.

Almost as cherished as the eternal controversy as to the identity of Shakespeare himself is the lesser speculation about the connection between Fastolfe and Falstaff. The real man who cast his great shadow over Southwark and Bermondsey died at the age of 82 in 1459, having enriched himself in the neighbourhood of Horselydown. He has been described as "one-third warrior, one-third shrewd man of the world, one-third knave." One of his foremost trading interests was in fish, an activity which is commemorated to this day in Pickle Herring Street, London S.E.1, which connects the Horselydown area with the Courage headquarters on Bankside. Fastolfe's interest in the fishing industry so prospered that he built himself an immense castle on the Norfolk coast at Caister. Each side of this stately home was 300 feet long with a large tower at each end of its corners, one of them a 100 feet high. It was well enough fortified to withstand a seige.

In London his home was in Stoney Street, between the two existing Courage Breweries, and formerly the Romans' road leading to their ferry across the Thames before London Bridge was built. Here Fastolfe lived in palatial style, sometimes with royalty as guests, and with William of Worcester, the chronicler, as one of his retainers. This William, on one occasion, recorded that "the Parliament being dissolved, the King Henry VI, held the feast of Christmas at Leicester; but

James Ormond, Count of Wiltshire, remained at the same feast at the house of Sir John Fastolfe in Southwark." Much of Horselydown came into the possession of Sir John, whose activities included money-lending, and whose nature – as many contemporary records show – was rapacious and acquisitive. Nearly 400 deeds relating to his possessions in the area went after his death to Magdalen College, Oxford – one of his beneficiaries. These included beer-houses, water-mills and gardens.

John Courage's acquisition, the former Knight's Hous, appears to have been among Fastolfe's possessions. Evidently it had become known as the Manor House after the knights had relinquished their use of it. Then it had developed into a place of entertainment, a great river-side beer-house with a laid out garden. In the reign of Edward IV it was mentioned in Chancery Proceedings as the "High Biere-howse and gardeyn, lately known as ffastolfe's". A picture by Hoefnagle, now at Hatfield House shows a fete at Horselydown in 1590, with the Tower of London across the Thames in the background and the great beer-house itself shown in full festive activity, in the true tradition of Southwark as a place of entertainment.

But on one occasion at least violence was visited upon the area in general and Sir John Fastolfe in particular. When Jack Cade was marching on London, Sir John filled his Southwark palace with armed veterans from his campaigns in France and fortified it with munitions of war. As a member of the King's Council he was prepared to resist the rebellion. He was prudent enough, however, to send forth one of his servants, a certain Payne, to enquire of Captain Cade, then encamped at Blackheath, what his intentions were. Payne was roughly handled, treated as a spy and threatened with death. Finally he was sent back with the message that "Sir John's House in Southwark shall be burned down and all his tenuries." Sir John was not a violent warrior. Hall's *Chronicles* recording the battle of Patay during the disastrous French campaigns had noted: "From this battle departed without any stroke stricken Sir John Fastolfe the same year for his valiantness elected into the Order of the Garter." Characteristically, therefore, Fastolfe listened to Payne and departed with all his followers from Southwark, which briefly became the headquarters of Cade before his death and failure of the rebellion. When it was all over Fastolfe returned to his possessions without apparently loss of face and certainly without diminishment of wealth. History treated him kindly and soon after John Courage arrived at Horselydown a biography of Sir John was published in which it was stated: "The streams of his treasure that fed the fountain of his munificence were numerous and plentiful . . . Sir John Fastolfe, the brave experienced soldier, the wise and able statesman, the steady patriot, the generous patron, the pious benefactor."

William Shakespeare could not have gone long unaware of Sir John Fastolfe when he arrived in Southwark from Stratford in 1586 – four years before the fete portrayed on Horselydown at which he may well have been present. The Knight had died well over a century before; but his name and reputation lingered on in the district and his doing had been well established in the chronicles from which Shakespeare took so much source material. So the immortal Falstaff owed his name in part, some of his character and much of his background, to the Fastolfe who had once proprietorily strutted Horselydown with brewing one of his local interests and the site of the first Courage brewhouse one of his many stakes in fifteenth century Southwark.

Whether Shakespeare himself made his home in Southwark has never been discovered. That he made his fame and fortune there as actor, playwright and playhouse proprietor is certain. Because playhouses, bear gardens and other places of entertainment were not permitted within the boundaries of the City of London, those in search of pleasure crossed the Thames to Southwark which had enjoyed a reputation for the frivolities of life since the days before Chaucer had celebrated them. Stow's *Survey of London* published at the time when Shakespeare was in full activity refers to the stews and shady establishments luring those who approached by boat from the City, advertising with "signes on their frontes, towardes the Thames, not hanged out, but painted on the walles, as a Beares Heade, the Crosse Keyes, the Gunne, the Castle, the Crane, the Cardinals Hatte, the Bell, the Swanne ..." Stow also wrote of the Bankside bear gardens in 1598: "there be the two Beare-gardens, the old and the new places wherein be kept Beares, Bulles, and other beastes, to be bayted. As also Mastiues in Seuerall kenels are there nourished to bait them. These Beares ... are ... bayted in plottes of grounde, scaffolded about for the beholder to stand safe."

Philip Henslowe and Edward Alleyn, founder of Dulwich College, were both in the bear-baiting business though it is as pioneers of the theatre associated with Shakespeare that they are mostly remembered. Indeed a Bankside carpenter named Gilbert Katherens undertook to build the Hope in 1613 as a "game place or plaiehouse fitt and convenient in all things both for players to plaie in and for the game of Beares and bulls to be bayted in the same ..."

The Rose, the Hope, the Swan and, most renowned of all, the Globe were the playhouses that arose and flourished in Shakespeare's day. The structure of the Globe had originally served as a playhouse at Shoreditch, another site outside the City of London boundaries favoured for theatrical presentations. In 1598 the lessees, Richard Burbage and others, were forced to move out of Shoreditch, pull down their theatre and transport "all the wood and timber thereof unto the Banckside in the parishe of St. Marye Overyes, and there erect a newe playhouse with the sayd timber and woode." The Globe was built on a plot in yhr Maid Lane, Southwark, now occupied by the Courage bottling plant. It was opened in July 1599 by the Lord Chamberlain's men and managed by Burbage. Many of Shakespeare's plays including *King Henry V, King Richard II, As You Like It, Romeo & Juliet* and *Julius Caesar* had their first performances there (Globe first nights were in the afternoons). Shakespeare himself was connected with the Globe not only as a playwright and actor but also as a shareholder. The original lease which shows the Burbage family to have had the main interest also refers to Shakespeare by name. During the production of one of his works in June 1613 the letting off of stage effects set fire to the building. "The burning of the *Globe,* or Playhouse on the *Bankside,* on St. *Peter's* Day," wrote a contemporary, "fell out by a Peale of *Chambers* (that I know not upon what Occasion were to be used in the Play), the *Tamplin* or *Stopple* of one of them lightin in the Thatch, that covered the House, burn'd it down to the Ground in less than two Hours, with a Dwelling-house adjoyning, and it was a great Marvaile and fair Grace of God, that the People had so little Harm, having but two narrow Doors to get out." It was immediately rebuilt and opened again in 1614, but Shakespeare hardly knew this new theatre for he died two years later.

The Southwark playhouses continued to thrive until they were closed down by Cromwell. When the Restoration came, London's theatrical life was re-established north of the Thames, leaving Southwark to less sophisticated entertainments such as baiting and prize-fighting. Samuel Pepys enjoyed the pleasures of the beer gardens in the summer of 1666 and in September of that year stopped at a little ale-house in Southwark from which he witnessed the great fire of London: "a most horrid malicious bloody flame".

At the time of Pepys' visits to the south bank there was already a large community of refugees from religious persecution established in Southwark. They brought new talents and produced great wealth. They were particularly influential in the promotion of brewing. Flemings in particular brought with them great improvements to the trade, including the use of hops. Their breweries extended all along the foreshore from Bankside to Horselydown. Notable among them was Henry Leake, who founded St. Olave's Grammar School, and Vassal Weblyng or Webling. The latter had a contract in 1578 to supply beer to St. Thomas's Hospital. This he evidently fulfilled too generously for the Governors' records showed a complaint that "the house beer is too strong and begets a taste; the poor go abroad especially on Sabothe day, and abuse themselves in taverns and alehouses, to the great displeasure of Almighty God, and the misliking of the Governors; they take order that no strong beer shall be allowed, and none fetched except a pynte at a tyme, by order of the physician."

It has been suggested that Vassall Webling was one of the figures portrayed in Hoefnagle's picture of Horselydown. It seems almost certain that he came into possession of the Fastolfe breweries there and that the Webling brewing family was one of Courages' forerunners on the site of the brewery at Horselydown. A certain Nicholas Webling granted a messuage there called Fastolphes in 1611 but the Weblings had faded from the scene by the time John Courage arrived in the eighteenth century.

The Courage family continuity was at its most tenuous at the outset when John Courage died suddenly in 1793. His widow Harriot was left with a young family in which the only boy, John, was but three years old. At the time of his birth it had been the pious ambition of the Courages that this boy should be brought up to enter the church, while his three sisters were to be given an education befitting them for the new status in society into which their family had moved. But before the father's death the business was already thriving so well that it had been decided that little John should enter it in due course, after mingling perhaps with sons of other brewers whose entry into their family business was already recognised at that time to be by way of a good public school and university.

The Courage family at this time still lived on the brewery premises and the business was sufficiently small for Harriot to be familiar with the day-to-day management. Although it was many years before there was much talk of the emancipation of women the brewing industry, unlike most others, was never unamenable to female management. So Harriot took over as a matter of course and settled down to run the affairs of Horselydown with the help of her managing clerk John Donaldson until such time as her son should be ready to take over after receiving the education to which he was entitled.

For a few years Harriot Courage carried on, but in 1797 she died. There was no member of the Courage family to step into the management so John Donaldson took over. He was charged with the care of the young children and became a partner in the business, taking a third of the gross profits which was afterwards enlarged to half, as well as a half of the capital. Already

1. A robust exchange of letters between John Courage I and R. Rankin of Leadenhall Street. John Courage's reply was written on the back of the letter.

R. Rankin's letter (above)

Courage.
I understand you are affronted with me—
and as I like to meet such things in a fair and
manly manner : I think it but candid to
declare :.
If I have given offence it is unintentionall—if I
did not ask you to drink a glass of wine the
Sunday you called, it was from forgetfullness
not intention. If after this explanation you
continue youre I're
Be affronted and be Damn'd.

Leadenhall St. Mar 21-96
R. Rankin

John Courage's reply (below)

R.
You are too contemptable (for a man) to be
offended with. But you deserve no pity for
you ought to do us better. I know its beneath
me to use (from) you a quotation. But as it does
not suit Shad Thames I return it from whence
it came being more suitable to the original.
You may be affronted and be
Damn'd you Carnot

Sgd. Courage
21 Mar 96.

2. John Courage the First
(who founded the Courage
Brewery in 1787).

3. John Courage the Second
who entered Courage's
Brewery in 1804 and carried
on the business until his
death 50 years later.

4. Edward Courage who
entered the Brewery in
1856 and died in 1904.

3

4

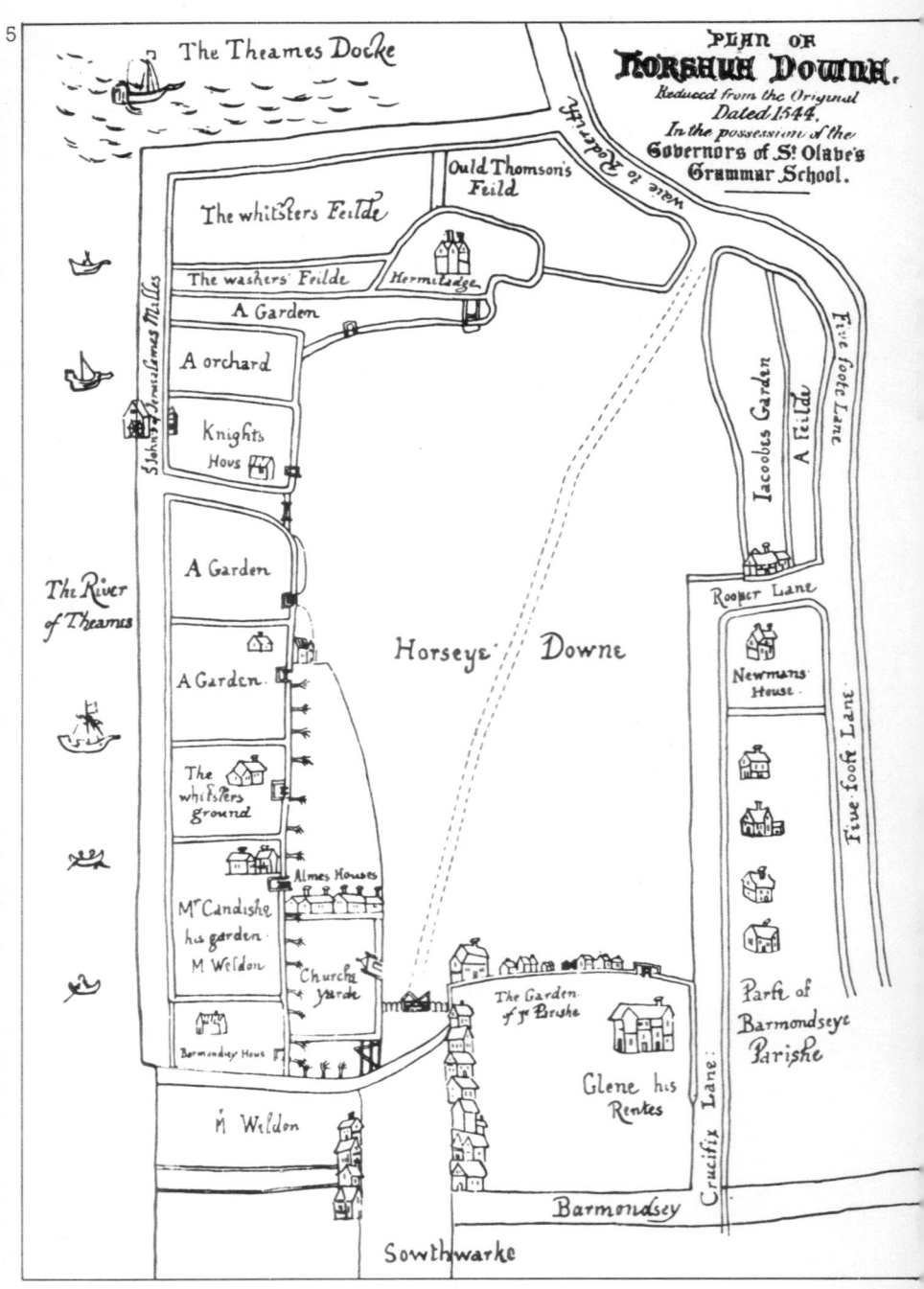

5

The Theames Docke

PLAN OF
HORSHUH DOWNH.
Reduced from the Original
Dated 1544.
In the possession of the
Governors of St. Olave's
Grammar School.

Ould Thomson's
Feild

The whitsters Feilde

Vale to Ratcliffe

The washers' Feilde

Hermitadge

A Garden

A orchard

Knights
Hous

St. Johns Thomas James Milles

Iacoobes Garden

A Feilde

Five foot lane

Rooper Lane

A Garden

Horseye Downe

Newmans
House

A Garden

Five foot Lane

The
whitsters
ground

The River
of Theames

Almes Houses

Mr Candishe
his garden
M Weldon

Church
yarde

The Garden
of ye Prishe

Parte of
Barmondseye
Parishe

Glene his
Rentes

Barmondsey Hous

M Weldon

Crucifix Lane

Barmondsey

Sowthwarke

5. Plan of Horselydown
dated 1544, where John
Courage later established
his Brewery.

6. Representation of a Fair
at Horselydown in 1590 with
the Thames in the back-
ground.

7. Horselydown Lane, 1947.

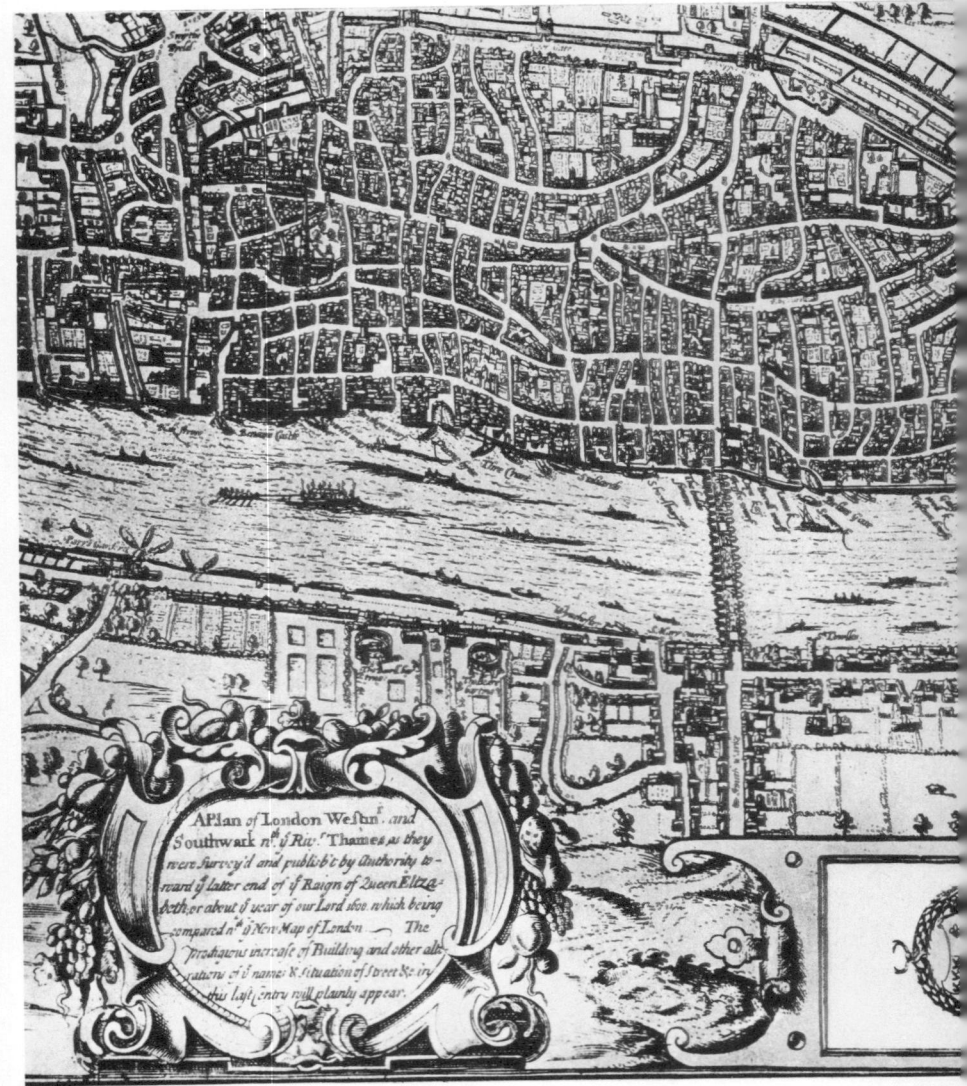

A Plan of London Westm^r. and Southwark n^r. y^e Riv^r. Thames, as they were survey'd and publish't by Authority toward y^e latter end of y^e Raign of Queen Eliza beth, or about y^e year of our Lord 1600. which being compared wth y^e New Map of London The prodigious increase of Building and other alterations of y^e names & situation of Street &c in this last Entry will plainly appear.

8. Early Plan of Horselydown.

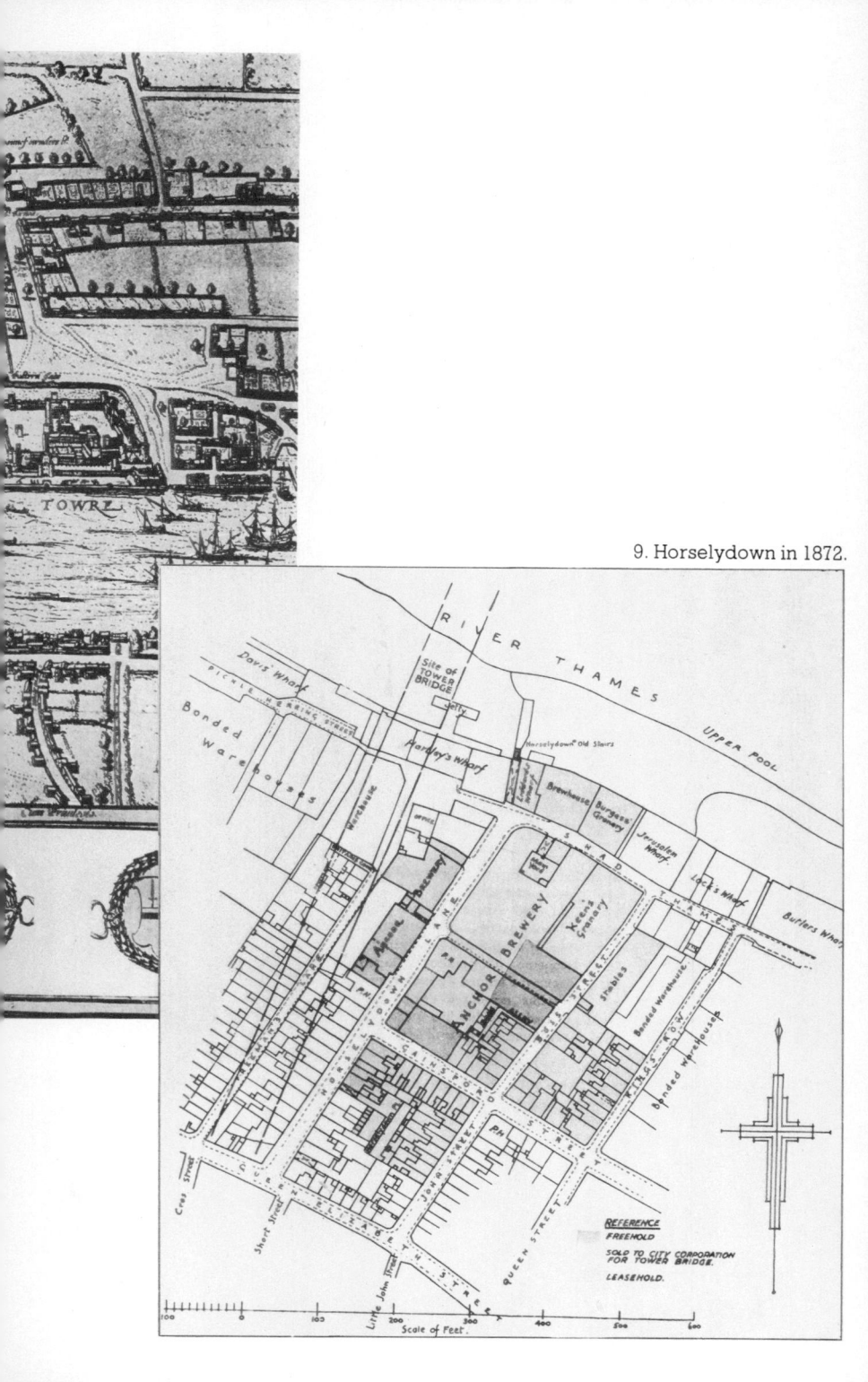

9. Horselydown in 1872.

10.Picture of Shad Thames in 1948 ; the little riverside highway which runs through the complex of the Anchor Brewery.

in 1800 the firm was described as Courage and Donaldson, Brewers, in the Post Office Directory, and it carried that title until 1851. There still exists in the brewery at Horselydown a key stone over an entrance inscribed "C. & D. 1847".

It was said that Donaldson was not over enthusiastic in his promotion of the children's education. But under his management the brewery flourished and the children were well looked after financially, money from the partnership being placed to the stock account of the Courage family. The young John Courage grew up under the shadow of the Napoleonic threat but within an industry which, unaffected by foreign affairs, was prospering through the application of new methods to traditional uses. By 1800 steam engines had been installed by Boulton & Watt in sixteen breweries, mainly in London. Industrial changes were also showing in the tideway which flowed by Horselydown. Steam was replacing sail. The coal barges multiplied. The cross-river wherries were being displaced by the Hackney cabs over the bridges. The stream itself was being polluted. Salmon had long since ceased to come up from the sea. The fishing of whitebait to be consumed in the riverside taverns was doomed. Belching chimneys decorated the crowded Southwark skyline. The more prosperous citizens were leaving Southwark to commute from the healthier climates of Camberwell and Dulwich.

The education of John the Second was not prolonged. He entered the brewery at the age of 14 on an initial salary of £60 a year, which in those times was handsome. He became a partner on attaining his majority in 1811. His sisters Ann, Elizabeth and Harriet meanwhile were each credited with £2,000.

The partnership between John Donaldson and the young John Courage continued for some twenty five years. That it was prosperous is indicated by the fact that the nominal estate was valued at £151,215 after writing off losses and appreciation when John Donaldson retired in 1836. In less than fifty years the value of the business had increased two hundredfold and the buildings at Horselydown had multiplied. John the Second married into brewing. His wife, Susan, was the daughter of a

Norfolk brewer, Sidney Hawes, and she gave him ten children. The Courages did not live in Southwark but set up their first home in De Crespigny Terrace, Camberwell, later moving to Dulwich.

There was another generation of Donaldsons in the business. On John Donaldson's retirement his interests were taken over by his son, Thomas, who took 5/12ths of the profits leaving 7/12ths for John Courage. Five years later a second Donaldson son, Robert, was taken into partnership but this evidently proved unsatisfactory for he retired after only five years. In 1848 Thomas Donaldson died intestate and for a few years his widow carried his share of the business. In 1851 the Donaldsons' participation ended. By agreement John Courage took £84,511 and Mrs. Donaldson £70,591 of the capital. By the age of sixty-one, after forty years experience of the business, John the Second became the sole ruler at Horselydown. Though the partnership had shown good returns, its ending came as a relief. G. N. Hardinge, Managing Director of Courages Brewery 1897–1927 wrote that John Courage "had been yoked as a partner solely through his own kindness to his father's employee, to a family whose members had done exceedingly well for themselves at his expense."

John the Second who lived until 1854 was the real consolidator of the business. When the first John Courage made his initial brew of 50 barrels his property consisted of the small brewhouse and its foreshore. During his short reign and his son's long one, the physical boundaries spread both east and west along the foreshore. This was the period when the brewing industry discovered the high value of waterborne transport. At the beginning of the nineteenth century, roads were generally scandalous, and transport within the cities slow and congested. Though steam was coming into industry and shipping, the railroads did not open up until the middle of the century. It is significant therefore, that John the Second acquired Liddards and Hartley's Wharves to the west and Burgess's and Keen's Wharves to the east. Much property was being acquired inland along Horselydown Lane but the river frontage was all-important and this extended to the west over the site of the approaches to Tower Bridge. The Corporation of London bought some of this property when the bridge was built in the eighteen-eighties.

The wharves in those days were busy with the intake of malt, coal, timber and forage for the horses. Ales were loaded off into barges for movement on the Thames and for transfer to ships plying to Lowestoft, Dundee and Leith. Soon there were consignments of stout for the Continent. The river played such an important part in the working of the brewery that the firm retained its own lightermen and barges. For the partners on their frequent journeys across to the City of London there was the firm's skiff called "The Brothers". Before the building of Tower Bridge most of those who had business with the firm, including of course the Excise Officers, came and went by water. For those who cherish romantic memories of the busy Thames tideway such as that painted by Canaletto and Turner, and familiar to Shakespeare and Dickens, it is somewhat sad that the traffic of the great brewery has turned its back on the waterfront. In common with other great riverside breweries throughout the British Isles, the Courage Group now relies upon road and rail transport even for consignments destined to be shipped overseas.

The fact that the breweries had been so often sited on the banks of rivers has nourished the popular fiction that beer, ale and stout owe their special qualities to the rivers beside which they had been brewed. Undoubtedly the early brewers of Southwark drew on the Thames for their water supply but as the industry developed, depending always on waterways for transport, nearly every great brewery possessed its own wells. John the Second sunk a well in the brewhouse which yielded more than enough water for his needs, and supplied the demands of many of his neighbours. Similar old wells with abundant supplies are to be found in the other main breweries of the Courage Group, at Bankside, Reading and Bristol. Peter

Mathias, writing specifically on the subject of porter brewing, refers to "the myth that porter derived its quality from the inimitable Thames water used to make it." His remarks applied equally to other products of breweries: "From the first, writers pointed out that most porter breweries drew their liquor from wells or the New River rather than the Thames, but the tenacity of the belief was proof against such factual refutations. In Ireland, a similar myth about the Liffey water has survived logical rebuttal down to our own day. Its charm is that of the real folk-myth, which gives an irrational explanation to a true perception, and its significance for later times, similarly is the admission of inferiority through an incorrect but wishful thought. The myth reflected the envy and frustration of provincial brewers prevented by their smaller scale of production and lesser skill, from achieving the increments in quality given by large-scale porter brewing."

The significance of the water supply had been seen by the first John Courage when he purchased the property which includes the wells which had originally served the knights of St. John. That John the Second had done much to improve them is indicated by Alfred Barnard's account of a visit to the brewery in 1889: "Beneath the stone-paved floor is the artesian well, so celebrated in Horselydown, and a great boon to the families in the locality, who have free access to it in the summer time. The water of this well is noted for its purity and coldness, hence the place is literally besieged in June, July and August. It is sunk to a total depth of 450 feet from the surface, and the first 100 feet is lined with cylinders 7 feet in diameter; after that the bore pipes on the Thames side, which are sunk to the depth of 350 feet, are of a 9-inch bore; but on the land side they are only sunk to the depth of 250 feet, and 18 inches in diameter. It yields 200 barrels per hour of the most splendid water for brewing or domestic purposes to be obtained in the south of London."

John the Second achieved not only consolidation of the business but also of the dynasty which bears his name. A year after the Donaldson partnership had dissolved, he took into partnership his two older sons, John and Robert, each being credited with £500 of capital and allocated 1/8th of the profits. Thus, in 1852 the business became wholly a family concern. Two years later John the Second died intestate and John the Third began a brief reign, with his brothers Robert and Edward as partners. After his death another, Henry, was admitted into the partnership in 1869. A younger brother, Alfred, was financed to set up in a malt business which, as Tomkins & Courage, became closely associated with the brewery. In 1882 there was a final change in the partnership when Robert's son entered into it; then in April 1888 the Courage family partnership, having existed for just over a century, came to an end with the formation of the limited company Courage & Co.

In that same year as it happened, Alfred Barnard, writing his account of "Noted Breweries" which was published in four volumes, visited Horselydown and we have his picture of the concern as it became a limited company in the heyday of Victorian prosperity. He was received by John Watt who was typical of the trusted managerial staff of the period. He was then Company Secretary having entered the firm's employment in 1847. His father, who had joined the firm in 1814, had been the right-hand man of John the Second, so the Watts between them – while never achieving the status of partners – had played a very significant part in the building of the enterprise.

With the second John Watt as his guide, Alfred Barnard recorded these glimpses of the brewery at work. It covered nearly four acres:

"The buildings on the south side of Shad Thames are devoted to the fermenting department, stores, cooperages, counting-house, and offices, and, with the exception of the latter, are comprised in the oldest part of the property. The brewhouse proper is a noble and lofty building, erected on the banks of the Thames, with a landing beach along its front for unloading the malt-ladened barges. It forms a conspicuous object from the river, and is situated nearly opposite the Tower of London." This of course was before Tower Bridge had been built.

There was no doubt about the use being made of Thames transport. "We ascended to the topmost floor of the building to see a delivery of malt elevated by a steam lift from the barges on the Thames, which is done very rapidly at the rate of 1,000 quarters per day."

The fermenting process of the day, already sophisticated sent Barnard into flights of maritime fancy: "When the ale is cooled by the refrigerating process, it is conveyed through a large main across the street at a great elevation into the finishing refrigerators in the big tun-room, which commands all the fermenting vessels, both porter and ale. As we stepped down from the bridge, we found ourselves in a lofty room, 63 feet by 40 feet, open to the roof. Before us appeared on either side a row of lofty vessels, leaving a 6-foot gangway, through which we walked. Running along the front, and fixed to some of the vessels, is a gallery 6 feet from the ground to enable the tunmen to get at the tuns for gauging purposes. Bearing round to the left of No. 5 vessel, we passed into the No. 2 room, which is a continuation of the first, and of the same lofty height. It measures 80 feet by 70 feet, is lighted by a dozen tall windows, and some of the fermenting vessels are 50 feet high. At the back of the first floor there is another row of similar vessels, but they are square. To surprise us, our guide conducted us up an exceedingly narrow staircase, thus enabling us to take a peep into Nos. 6 and 7, which are old-fashioned and square. We thought these capacious; but we were to be more astonished, for he next led the way between some vessels, where we could hardly pass along, to a narrow gangway, and then passing up a slanting plank we arrived at the top of the two most notable vessels, Nos. 11 and 12, which opened their yawning gulfs of ale beneath our feet. On the surface of either of these seas of ale a lifeboat could float, so great is their size. Like the other fermenting vessels, they contain boat skimmers for removing the yeast from the surface to a slate yeast-back below, where it is stored for pitching purposes in the brewery."

The brewery's transport arrangements were already a matter

of pride: "There is a stabling for seventy-nine horses and, besides these, several well-fitted and ventilated loose boxes. The splendid quadrupeds belonging to this firm are so well-known, that we need scarcely describe them. Mr. Lawson informed us that he purchased them chiefly in North Wales and Cheshire, and that he considers that breed of animals very clean, with plenty of bone, and healthy. Messrs. Courage's horses generally run $16\frac{1}{2}$ hands high, will draw two tons each, and cost on an average £80 a piece. Some of them took first prizes at the Olympia and Albert Palace Shows in 1887, and, in the year 1886, this firm took four first prizes at the Battersea Show . . ."

There are thirty-five vans in use by the firm – twenty large and fifteen small – the former are three-horse ones and will load up twenty-five barrels, and the latter fifteen. This is the busiest brewery, for its size, in London; and on the day of our visit 1,600 barrels were carted away from the establishment."

Finally, Barnard noted that twenty clerks were "constantly employed" in the offices, that the brewery employed two hundred men and that the output in the previous year had exceeded 300,000 barrels.

Barnard was in fact recording the finale of that Victorian scene. In May 1891 a spark in the malt mills caused an explosion which set light to the inflammable malt dust. The brewhouse burned for several days, engaging the attention of one of London's legendary firemen, Captain Eyre Massey Shaw who was not only a member of the Prince of Wales's social circle but was celebrated in song in the lines in *Iolanthe,* which ran:

> Oh, Captain Shaw,
> Type of true love kept under!
> Could thy Brigade
> With cold cascade
> Quench my great love, I wonder?

His cold cascades delivered from the new steam fire-engines in the streets and from tugs and floats on the river failed to save the brewhouse which was a total loss.

The powers of recovery at that time, however, were resilient. Brewing at Horselydown ceased only for about four weeks. Characteristic of the friendly relationships between rival breweries was the arrangement immediately made with Messrs. Barclay and Perkins to supply all the London Beers required by Courages to fulfill their commitments. The sum for this supply came to about £40,000. It was the first large collaboration between the two concerns which 65 years later were to merge.

Before the 1891 fire, Courages had already established working arrangements with other brewery concerns. The water from the Horselydown well was admirable for the traditional London beers such as mild ale and stout and, long before the family concern became a public company, the Courage London-brewed beers had become popular outside the metropolis and overseas. But at that time it was thought that the Southwark water lacked the mineral ingredients required for a good pale ale – the increasingly popular bitter. By the eighteen-seventies Courages recognised the need to supply their customers with these other types of beer to meet public demand. In 1872, therefore, they contracted with Flower & Son of Stratford-on-Avon, brewers of a fine beer, to supply them with pale ale for their own distribution.

This arrangement depended of course upon the Victorian transportation system which was already well established. The beer came from Stratford to London by rail. It was then carted across the Thames to the brewery where it was assembled for redistribution. Significantly the youngest of the family partnership, Robert Michell Courage, was taking what was then a forward-looking interest in the problems of logistics. Although railway freightage had been revolutionizing brewery distribution over several decades, he saw a means of simplifying the pale ale operation by reverting to water-transport. So in the late eighteen-eighties the pale ale contract was transferred to Fremlins of Maidstone, whose brewery was on the banks of the Medway. Thus the casks of bitter went by tall-masted brown-sailed barges direct from the Medway into the Thames and up the tideway to the Courage wharf at Shad Thames. At the height of this operation some 32,000 barrels a year sailed in this leisurely fashion.

The brown sails of these beer ferries lingered on into the present century but not for long. By 1903 there was a further rationalization. It was clear then that it was better business for a prosperous concern such as Courages to acquire the means of production, particularly in an age when distribution was becoming more sophisticated. Courages decided to brew their own bitter beers in some place outside London where the water was suitable, and they began a search for an existing business to acquire. Their acquisition of Messrs. G. & E. Hall's brewery at Alton in Hampshire was their first move outside London in the creation of the structure which has now become the Courage Group. It should perhaps be noticed that acquisition, merger and amalgamation – which in the contemporary term 'takeover' seems to represent so very much the idiom of this mid-century – has been almost a traditional element in the brewing industry.

After the early eighteenth century when brewing was entirely localised, popular demand and scientific methods created larger scale production and stablization of quality. This with improving means of distribution in the nineteenth century favoured larger units of production and throughout Victorian times there was a tendency for these larger units to take over the smaller breweries with their tied houses. Because of all the long term elements which make up a brewery concern, the tied houses, the maltings, the water supply and the local goodwill, it has always been more desirable to acquire an existing concern rather than to start an entirely new one. It is difficult to name a brewing concern at the present day which is not in some way rooted in the takeovers of the past.

The Alton brewery had been bought by Henry Hall in 1841 and it possessed a historical interest in that the Manager, when it was acquired by Hall, was a certain James Newman Frost, who was a relative and friend of John Henry Newman, and the Cardinal had frequently stayed at the Brewers House. During

26

the second half of the nineteenth century the brewery, deriving its exceptional qualities from the Alton wells, built up a substantial localized trade and its beers became well known in London. At the time of Courage's acquisition in 1903, the output amounted to 20,000 barrels a year. The Hall concern was typical of the well established country breweries of the period. It possessed its own maltings and its beers were largely brewed from Hampshire barley and hops. During the first decade of the present century Courages reconstructed the buildings and by the nineteen-thirties Alton was producing 4,000 barrels a week.

Alton continues to play an important part in the Courage Group. It is still in service but in these days of specialisation its main significance is as a Group canning and kegging plant. But for all the industrialisation of Alton, there lingers one noble aspect of the past which calls for a digression. Here, adjacent to the brewery, is the stable for the Courage dray-horses which, since the beginning of the nineteen-fifties have moved out of London to a neat well furnished Hampshire home. It is now acknowledged that there is no useful place for the brewer's horse-drawn dray in this mechanised age. Courages still had fourteen working horses in London in 1951 when it was decided that horse-drawn vehicles were no longer commercially viable.

Fortunately, the splendour of the turn-out was recognised as something to be preserved not only for sentiment but for prestige and publicity purposes. So there remain at Alton six shire bay geldings with a noble dray in the Courage livery painted in maroon and gold. The team is maintained from new stock when occasion arises. Compared with their forerunners these great horses, each more than 17 hands, are much travelled. They go, by motor, all over the country to take part in parades and show events.

They serve as a reminder not only of the pride and glory of the past but also of the extent to which the breweries – more than most industrial enterprises – continued to rely very heavily on the services of the horses long after railways and even mechanised road transport were well established. For instance, in 1893 W. J. Gordon in *The Horse-World of London* saw the Courage horse as a permanent feature of London life: "The brewer's horse is a splendid animal, the most powerful as a rule of London's heavy brigade. At the Cart-horse Parade, in which teams of all classes compete, the first second, and third prizes were taken for the only two years in which they entered by Messrs. Courage, whose cart horses are generally sold for an average of £32 each, one of them having fetched fifty-one guineas, the highest price ever obtained for a horse cleared out of a stud as being past the work of the trade in which he made his first appearance in town. In fact, there is no stud in the kingdom of higher level excellence than that under Mr. Laird's care at Horselydown, which is saying much, considering that the 3,000 horses owned by the larger London brewers are worth at the very lowest estimate £90 apiece.

"A barrel of beer weighs 4 cwt; a brewer's van carries 25 barrels, which means 5 tons; the van itself weighs not less than 35 cwt., some of them weigh over 2 tons; the harness weighs three quarters of a hundred-weight; the men weigh – what? It is a delicate question. To answer it Mr. Laird weighed a drayman for us, a fine young man in his twenty-ninth year. He weighed 20 st. 10 lbs! And the horse he drove, a five-year-old gelding standing 17.2 and still growing, was then put on the scale, and dipped the beam at just over the ton.

"But this is hardly a fair average. Let us throw the men in with the sundries, and say these tremendous horses have to draw 8 tons; and this is for three horses worked unicorn fashion, two at the pole and one as leader. According to one horse-keeper, who had been twenty-seven years in his position, it now takes three horses to do the work that four did twenty years ago. 'The vans have improved, the roads have improved, and the horses have improved, especially the horses'."

When the Courage company was formed in 1889 the stud consisted of 78 heavy draft horses. In 1914 the stud had been increased to 104. The first large garage was erected at Horsely-down in 1920 "to meet the new methods of delivery".

Mechanization of transport was in fact the most significant aspect of the development of the brewing industry in the first three decades of this century, but the changes came slowly for the horse remained for so long the most economical form of transport for the short journeys with frequent stops entailed in delivery rounds. There was also – and this happily remains to this day – a feeling of pride and affection for the splendid horses associated with the trade. Henry Courage devoted himself to this side of the business in the early part of the century. His aim was for the firm to have the best horses on the road, and in this there was keen competition with other great breweries. The Courage teams were arranged in colour. His pride was the unicorns of three matched horses pulling a dray loaded with six tons of beer through the crowded streets of London. The family interest in transportation remained strong for he was succeeded by his son, H. Ernest Courage, and by the thirties when mechanization was almost complete the transport system came under supervision of Captain J. H. Courage.

But the transport revolution, which afterwards had such a potent effect upon the building up of the structure of the Group, was essentially gradual. Although the First World War had seen the disappearances of cavalry and the virtual elimination of horse-drawn vehicles for military purposes in favour of petrol driven power, many of the brewery concerns while retaining their horses turned their attention first to steam. The first mechanical vehicle purchased by Courages was a steam Foden bought in 1916 for £673, and between the wars the Foden steamers were a popular form of brewery transport which are still nostalgically remembered by older people and, when they can be found, collected by veteran enthusiasts. Courages purchased their first Commer car during the First World War and in 1920 their first K type Leyland motor lorry which cost £1,310. By 1930 they were running 34 Leylands, 5 Fodens, 5

Morris Trucks, and 3 Trailers, and there was still a stud of 32 horses.

A development which brought new pressure on the transport system early in the present century was the new popularity of bottled beers. At the turn of the century the tied-houses belonging to such concerns as Courages had a free hand to make their own arrangements for bottled beers. At that time the only large brewers who were bottling to any extent were Messrs. Whitbreads.

To meet the growing popular demand for bottled beer with their own resources, Courages made their first move in 1904 by coming to an arrangement with the Star Bottling Company to supply their houses. When this did not succeed they contracted with various London firms – Messrs. M. B. Foster for Bass and Guinness, Messrs. R. P. Culley & Co. for Worthington and Guinness, and Messrs. Fremlin Bros. for all the lighter brands. This somewhat cumbersome arrangement weighed heavily on the transport system for the goods had to be collected by the brewery and special staff engaged to superintend deliveries. Bottling trade in fact increased so rapidly that Courages erected their own plant just before the First World War. By 1930 they were running a fleet of 27 bottled beer vans and lorries. In that year their output of bottled beers was some 54,000 barrels a year which represented about 25 per cent of the brewery's output.

From the times of John the Second the Courage policy had been to regard itself as a public-house, rather than a family trade concern. This had meant an ever increasing involvement in what may be loosely termed as "tied-houses". This involvement from the last century into this has been described by G. N. Hardinge: "The firm's method of dealing with its public house customers had been the loan method. Its practice was to lend money to business on mortgage of the freeholds or leaseholds of their houses. The pursuit of this method at one time led to the firm's ceasing membership of Brewers' Hall, which was enforcing restrictive regulations upon its members on the question of loans. To Courages it seemed best that the Brewery should have a free hand in the matter. As a result of maintaining this policy a very large number of public houses came within the scope of their trade. They would make the licensee a loan on first charge which advance he would usually follow up by a second loan from Pale Ale brewers, such as Bass's, Worthington's or Allsopp's, who thus got the Pale Ale trade, and by a third charge loan from distillers, who thereby secured the spirit trade – the licensee himself finding the balance of the needed capital. Under this system Courage's outstanding loans would be at times as high as a million sterling; the actual figure in 1887, for example, was £955,675. That was during the days when the business was still a partnership.

"A few years later much higher figures were attained. In the late Nineties came the great boom in the brewing trade. Cheap money and the lending of large sums by Banks and Investment and Insurance Companies, and competition among Brewers for the purchase of houses, were the features of the time, and the high prices which in consequence were commonly paid can certainly be described as inflated.

"With Courages the new development meant a further big increase in their loans, which in 1897 reached the colossal figure of £2,202,879, and in that year the output reached 333,400 barrels. To meet these heavy financial engagements fresh capital was issued, and the Company bought a large number of houses; and though it withstood the prevalent temptation to pay almost any price for properties, it nevertheless did pay some very high figures. Later this inflated finance of the Trade had the unfortunate result of drawing the attention of the Chancellor of the Exchequer to a further source of revenue."

Like other great breweries, Courages became virtually bankers to a host of licensed victuallers in the areas in which they were operating which were ever wider as the business grew and the efficiency of transport increased. It was, and still is, an extremely personal business. It was uniquely personal in the case of one George Wyatt, a big man in business in a big way.

He weighed well over 20 stone and, as a publican he controlled some fifteen houses for the promotion of which he needed the sizable sum of £100,000. The Courage directors of the period were impressed by Wyatt's keenness and acumen but regarded the size of the operation as something of a risk, and therefore sought an endowment policy for a large sum on his life. The Insurance company demanded that Wyatt be weighed, but sufficient weights could not be found and hefty office ledgers had to be brought in to balance him on the scales. The precaution turned out to be unnecessary for Wyatt continued to prosper and outlived the policy.

After the turn of the century the Company's loans decreased and the policy of taking over ownership increased. Thus in 1900 the Company's loans stood at just under £2 million while their estates were valued at about £950,000. By 1930 this balance was reversed – the loans standing at about £350,000 and the value of the estates having built up to well over £2½ million.

Throughout all the developments which carried the company through its formation in the eighteen-eighties into the present century, the Courage family continuity was maintained. Robert Courage was the company's first chairman from 1886 to 1893. He was succeeded by Edward Courage who steered the company with a firmly conservative policy through the inflationary period at the turn of the century until his death in 1904. He always maintained that dividends should never exceed 10 per cent, and this policy paid off when legislation brought fresh taxation on brewers and many public houses were depreciated in value. He had built up large reserves which were used to meet depreciation at a time when other breweries were forced to write down their share capital.

He was succeeded by his son, Raymond Courage, who continued the policy during the period before the First World War when drink legislation was hitting the brewery trade particularly hard. Lloyd George's Finance Act, 1910, heavily increased license duties. Until that time the license duty for a public house had been £10 above 10% of its gross assessment, with a maximum of £60 per annum. The Act increased this to 50% of the gross assessment, with various other increases. The license duty of the Courage houses rose from £3,000 to £30,000 a year, making a further depreciation of £27,000 a year to be met. Again this was a case where other companies wrote down their capital, but Raymond Courage insisted that the £100 ordinary shares issued by the company should remain at £100 and that depreciation must be met out of income. This was a thin time for the shareholders, practically all members of the Courage family, for between 1910 and 1913 the dividend dropped to 1%.

The First World War of course brought massive drink legislation, a Beer Tax in 1914, restricted opening hours for public houses in 1915, restriction of output amounting to rationing in 1916, and restrictions in the average gravity of all beers in 1917 and 1918. At Horselydown Courages, their staff depleted by war service, raised a Company of Special Constables and provided makeshift air-raid shelters in the cellars. Residents of Bermondsey whose parents used to come to draw water from the Horselydown wells now came to bed down on the hop pockets when the raiders came by night.

The business emerged unscathed to welcome a wave of prosperity which followed the war. It was still under the guidance of Raymond Courage as Chairman, and during this period there was remarkable intensity of family management. Commander A. V. Courage was Director in charge of production and the maintenance and improvement of public houses. Ernest Courage was Director responsible for transport. Oswald Courage was a Director principally concerned with the buying of materials, hops, etc. Captain J. H. Courage assisted the Commander in the general management of the public houses and M. V. Courage assisted him – these two being responsible for interviewing all applicants for public houses since it was a rule that all applicants should be passed by a Director of the Company. In addition, Colonel M. R. F. Courage was in charge of the brewery at Alton and the houses attached to it.

33

At Horselydown the acquisition of freehold interest gave the company a free hand to carry out an ambitious rebuilding scheme which was carried out from 1925 onwards. It is significant that at that time the wooden cask was regarded not only as traditional but as permanent. A steam cooperage which had been instituted after the fire of 1891 was reinstalled, and G. N. Hardinge in his account of the brewery in 1932 states that: "the company makes all its own casks and buys its own timber". By the nineteen sixties not a single cask was being made at Horselydown or indeed throughout the many breweries in the Courage Group. Steel had taken over.

The prosperity of the nineteen-twenties stemmed from the relaxation of war restrictions on output, a renewal of appetite for the pleasures of life, and a change from the attitude of people toward public houses and drinking. There was a more liberal attitude in social behaviour, a betterment of standards and a removal of the more squalid aspects of drinking which had lingered on since the nineteenth century. It was a period of much rebuilding and improvement in public houses. Much of the war time legislation and taxation remained. Indeed, the taxation of beer had continued to rise since the formation of the company. Beer duty in fact rose 16 fold between 1889 and 1920.

Nevertheless, Courages forged ahead by adapting to the new mood of the times by industrial reorganisation, by developing new amenities and by extending the whole pattern of the business.

The first expansion was north of the Thames, the acquisition of the Camden Brewery in Camden Town. The purchase was decided by the toss of a coin. Colonel John Courage and Charles Perkins, then representing rival concerns, were both interested parties in that they had both acquired seats on the board with an eye to future prospects. When a change of ownership became inevitable they did not bid against each other but settled by spinning. The concern formed into a public company in 1889, the same year as Courages, had an output of

42,000 barrels a year supplying 78 of their own houses. It had been founded in 1859 and its heavy gravity beers were well established throughout the north-west side of London, a district where Courages at that time were scarcely represented and its beer unknown. After the takeover the superintendence, collection and division of houses were kept separate within the Courage business, and friendly rivalry was fostered between the Courage interests north and south of the Thames.

The other expansion in the nineteen-twenties was a rural one consolidating the Alton business. In 1927 Courages acquired the Farnham United Breweries Company on the Surrey/Hampshire border. With it went a holding of 196 licensed houses. Its output amounted to 45,000 barrels a year and it possessed its own maltings. In 1969 these were sold to the Farnham Maltings Association an organisation of local citizens for conversion to a Community Centre.

The Farnham Brewery was itself typical of the nineteenth century concerns which built up through amalgamation. In 1839 two brothers, Robert and John Barrett who were hop growers in that district renowned for its hop gardens, began a small enterprise which they named the Red Lion Brewery. For a decade or so it served the needs of the immediate agricultural community. Then the impact of wars made itself felt in this rural scene. At the end of the Crimean War the British Government bought a tract of land for the creation of a permanent army camp. Thus in 1856 began the military settlement of Aldershot. In that year there were only two publicans in the village of Aldershot. Three years later there were already twenty fully-licensed houses and forty beer houses. The opportunist who had most energetically cashed in on the army construction programme was a local hop grower and property owner named George Trimmer. He built a brewery at Farnham and immediately applied for licences in Aldershot entering into fierce competition with the Barretts. In fact every time the Barretts got a petition signed for a beerhouse to serve the ever increasing military population, Trimmer would obtain one next door or opposite. The struggle later caused redundancy and the closing of certain houses by the Magistrates.

The Barretts did well enough with their enterprises in Aldershot, however, to expand in other directions. In 1866 they bought two small breweries with some twenty houses in the Basingstoke area. Their conflict with Trimmer resolved itself in 1889 when they joined forces to form Farnham United Breweries Company Limited with both families represented on the board. The Red Lion Brewery was closed down and the Farnham Brewery supplied the requirements of the united trade until Courages acquired it. Then the whole business was transferred to the Alton Brewery where the trade, after much rebuilding, had reached 120,000 barrels by the end of the twenties.

By the beginning of the nineteen-thirties, therefore, the Courage enterprise was established as a metropolitan concern with London breweries north and south of the Thames allied with a substantial and widespread interest spread over Surrey and Hampshire and centred at Alton.

4

The nineteen-thirties opened for the brewers under a cloud of huge and increasing unemployment and an emergency budget raising the taxation of beer; it closed with the Second World War and a string of new restrictions. Nevertheless the management of the Courage enterprise through the difficult years following the First World War had established it in such a position of strength that the policy of further expansion was possible and indeed desirable. The Company might have been deterred from this by the 1931 taxation described by Mr. Hardinge as "killing the consumption of the national beverage". Fortunately, as it turned out, the expansion had taken place the year before. In 1930 Courages acquired Noakes Brewery, a concern with a pattern somewhat similar to their own, having interests on the south bank of the Thames and also in the home counties west of London which, at that time, were in the throes of a massive residential and industrial expansion.

The Noakes business can be traced back to one of the ancient beer-houses which flourished when there were still fairs at Horselydown. For some two hundred years there was a brewery known as the Black Eagle in Crucifix Lane, the earliest record of any proprietor being a certain Clarke. An eighteenth century drawing depicts an eagle standing on a barrel engraved with the words: "Clarke's pure Bermondsey Ale. From malt and hops. Brewhouse, White's grounds, Bermondsey."

Those who lived and brewed in Bermondsey in those days still enjoyed kinship with the country. Adjoining the Black Eagle Brewery were the kennels of the Old Surrey Foxhounds described as the most ancient pack in Surrey. In 1750 it is recorded that their Master was Mr. Gobsall who was succeeded by Mr. Dudin, who moved the kennels from Bermondsey to Godstone toward the end of the eighteenth century. Green coats and beaver hats were the costume of the hunt and in those days it is recorded that they did not draw after 1 o'clock "so that the City men might be on 'Change by four". It was no doubt these City men who provided material for the writings of Surtees who, in his young days was studying law in London, hunted with the Surrey packs; and experience which led to the creation of Jorrocks. When the hunt moved the brewery took over the property and made use of the stables and kennels for these were still in existence in 1896, when the brewery was rebuilt.

After Clarke the next proprietor at the beginning of the nineteenth century was John Cox. There is an engraving advertising "Cox's Fine Double Strong Ale" dated 1837. A more general claim to fame for this brewer is that he is said to have originated the Cox's Orange Pippin. Maybe this was after he disappeared from the Southwark scene in 1848 when the brewery was sold to Messrs. Day, Payne & Co. The purchase price was £14,755 which included the freehold, plant, some nineteen houses together with book debts, rents and loans owing to the concern. The name Noakes first appeared in 1852 when Robert Day took as a partner Wickham Noakes. Thereafter the brewery was known for many years as Day, Noakes & Co., until it became a limited company in the eighteen-nineties.

Like Courages, the Noakes business had spread to the west of London. William Noakes, son or grandson of Wickham, had learned his brewing in the Nevile Reid Brewery at Windsor, and as chairman of his own concern he acquired the Windsor business in 1918 and also the Royal Brewery at Windsor in 1920. The latter was owned by the Canning family and possessed twenty houses. On the original site of the Noakes Brewery at Windsor under the shadow of the castle walls was erected the Lutyens memorial to George V.

In late 1937 Courages also acquired the Kidd Brewery at Dartford, Kent, thus spreading their interests to the east of London.

With the approach of the Second World War the Courage pattern of business had been rationalised on an industrial basis with the brewing at Horselydown and Alton and a depot at Windsor. The important industrial change which had taken place in the years between the wars was the movement of beer from barrel to bottle. By 1939 30 per cent of all beer consumed was sold in bottles. During this period the price of draught beer remained steady at about 4d for mild and 7d a pint for bitter in a public bar – in spite of rising costs of labour, transport and materials. Socially there had been a significant change in attitudes toward drinking and in drinking behaviour. Many pubs had been rebuilt, not always alas in the best of taste, to accommodate a wider range of customers who took their refreshment more comfortably and less furtively. To meet the population explosion around Greater London, many new pubs were also built.

During the years preceding the outbreak of the war and during the war itself it was recognised that beer was not a frivolous luxury but one of the essential ingredients in morale. The brewers worked in harmony with each other and with the Government. Unlike the Germans who, in March 1943, stopped the production of beer completely, the brewers of this country managed to maintain a flow, although many of them were in vulnerable positions. Courages at Horselydown, for instance, only lost two days of production. They also managed to increase the scope of their business by the acquisition of Hodgsons Kingston Brewery in 1943.

The overall war picture has been well recorded by H. A. Monckton of Messrs. Flower & Sons in his book A History of English Ale & Beer:- "The wartime and post-war Governments looked upon the supply of beer as a moral armament, and they made every effort to see that the people did not go without. Because of the unavoidable shortages of sugar and malting barley it was necessary to reduce the strength of beer considerably: far better to have sufficient quantity of beer at less strength. Even so, there were inevitable beer shortages, which meant that most licensed houses were restricted in the number of hours they had beer on sale. Once the weekly beer ration was exhausted the licensee was obliged to close his doors. However, the Brewers' Society 'Beer for Troops Committee' saw to it that serviceman had reasonable supplies. Beer in bottle, because of paper shortage left breweries without labels, and the only distinguishing feature between one beer and another was the colour of the metal closure. In the case of screw-stoppered bottles the distinction between one beer and another was by a small descriptive paper 'top strap'.

"For some five years after the War, the trade continued in the grip of severe restrictions which included a prohibition upon the repair of damaged breweries and the rebuilding of demolished public houses. Quite obviously the requirements of the licensed trade could not take priority over the rebuilding of war-damaged private houses, or factories upon whose output the country depended for its economic survival. Gradually these restrictions were loosened and beer duty also fell a little from its high level of 1949."

When the German bombardment began the ancient Boroughs of Southwark and Bermondsey were well in the target area, and the Horselydown brewhouse next to Tower Bridge was well in the centre of the target. In spite of the fact that the residential population of Southwark had been declining between the wars and war-evacuation had taken place, nearly a thousand people were killed by enemy bombardment. The brewery itself was hit. The roof of the brewhouse was completely stripped and the river wall was shattered. But the Victorian builders had done their job well and the old structure held the waters of the Thames.

Before the bombs fell the buildings at Horselydown, dating from the fire of 1891, were due for reconstruction. Owing to the post-war building restrictions the new brewhouse was not completed until 1954. In the following year two neighbours, who for some 200 years had been friendly rivals – sometimes in the tradition of the trade helping each other out in times of trouble – merged their interests. Courages joined forces with

Barclay Perkins of the famous Anchor Brewery just up river above London bridge. Generations of individuals from these two concerns have known each other well. The first John Perkins, for instance, must have been familar with John Courage the first and recognised a forthright man and a force to be reckoned with. In the history of Southwark and London brewing the interests of these two great concerns had always mingled. From 1955 they coincided to become a potent force. Something of the forthrightness of the first John Courage lingers on in his own handwriting now framed in Southwark Bridge Road: "You are too contemptable (for a man) to be offended with. But you deserve no pity for you ought to do us better. I know its beneath me to use (from) you a quotation. But as it does not suit Shad Thames I return it from whence it came being more suitable to the original. You may be affronted and be Damn'd you Carnot".

BARCLAY PERKINS

5

The Anchor Brewery, now administrative headquarters of
the Courage Group, had been, under various names and owner-
ships, an established feature of Southwark for several centuries
before Mr. David Barclay and Mr. John Perkins acquired
possession. Like Courage and Noakes, they took over a concern
which characteristically had changed hands through the years
but which had deep roots in the Borough's brewing tradition
which had mingled with literary history since the time of
Chaucer. Indeed, a bronze tablet let into a wall in Park Street
(unveiled by Sir Herbert Beerbohm Tree in 1909) records the
fact that the present brewery occupies the site of Shakespeare's
Globe Theatre.

It was a few years after the first Globe with its thatched roof
was burnt down that James Monger, a "Citizen and Cloth-
worker of London" started a brewhouse on a site adjoining the
rebuilt playhouse. It continued under the proprietorship of the
Mongers until 1665.

By the time the next owner, Josiah, sometimes called James
Child, appears, Shakespeare's playhouse had already vanished
but the Hope Theatre was still opening its doors in Southwark.

There were also doors in that neighbourhood which were
notoriously sinister, still commemorated in the name of Clink
Street which adjoins the present brewery buildings. "Clink"
became a synonym for all prisons everywhere because of the
reputation of the Clink Prison which Stow described as in-
carcerating "such as should brabble, frey or break the Peace on
the banke, or in the Brothell houses", but which was also used
for the imprisonment and execution of the victims of religious
persecution under both Mary and Elizabeth.

45

An entry in the public records in April 1666 states: "The King to the Brewer's Company, and recommends Josiah Child, merchant of London, who has done faithful service in supplying the navy with beer, and has bought a brewhouse in Southwark to brew for the household and navy, for admission as a free brother of the same company, for the same fee as the late Timothy Alsop the king's brewer paid . . ."

Like John Courage at Horselydown, Child fancied a nautical symbol because of his connection with shipping and during his ownership the brewhouse became known as the Anchor. He supplied the navy with masts, yards and bowsprits as well as stores and beer. His partner during this period, was a Bankside neighbour, John Shorter, who became Lord Mayor of London, and had John Bunyan – author of Pilgrim's Progress – as his unofficial Chaplain.

King Charles granted two brewing licenses to the Anchor in 1690 and these, with their bulky seals, have been preserved. By the turn of the century the concern was prospering. The Cash Bulletin for the years 1693 to 1702 shows sums varying from £40 to £100 a week paid to the Excise Authorities. A significant entry in the wages list was the name of Edmund Halsey who, at that time was drawing 20/-d a week. Halsey's was one of the most spectacular success stories in brewing. He was the son of a St. Albans miller who had come to seek his fortune in London after quarrelling with his father. He started at Southwark as a brewhouse labourer and thence rose to be Chief Clerk. No doubt, Josiah Child, much preoccupied with his shipping interests, regarded the brewery as just a useful diversification and was glad of the services of young Edmund Halsey to take the routine work off his hands.

In less than two years after his first appearance as a wage-earner, young Edmund had not only been taken into partnership but had married one of his master's daughters. From 1693 onwards he took over the business and ran it very efficiently. Regular sums of £100 a week, large amounts in those days, were paid to Excise Duty. In May 1695 both he and Child drew £400 each out of the business as distribution of profits. Edmund was a complete professional. Apart from his managerial salary he drew a further weekly sum as brewer. He was also wise to fringe benefits; his "rideing horse at the Livery Stables" was chargeable to the brewery.

Less than ten years after his first modest appearance at £1 a week in the firm's accounts, he was lending £1,000 to the King. As he prospered during the reign of William and Mary his expenditure, all carefully recorded, ranged from the shrewd to the lavish. In 1700, for instance, he lent small sums to Thomas Winnett and Richard Clarke – a marginal note explains that these were Excise Officers. He paid large sums for new coppers and buildings for the brewhouse and no doubt these included the extension of the business over the site of Shakespeare's playhouse. Significantly, in 1702 his personal expenditure included such items as "Man's livery, new sadle and bridle, wine for Hunt, long wigs and short wigs, shoes, shirts and books and schooling for Tho. Halsey".

He was in fact sole proprietor of the brewery until 1701. Child had died in 1696 leaving his interest to his widow, and Halsey paid a substantial weekly sum to his mother-in-law until her death. During the first decade of the century he amassed great wealth. During the second decade he established his social position. In 1710 he stood for Parliament but was defeated. When his opponent died, however, he was returned "in his room" and as Member for Southwark. This was challenged. In January 1711 there was a petition to the House complaining that Halsey's return had been achieved by bribery and other indirect practices and that it was due to the partiality of the High Bailiff. The House resolved "that Edmund Halsey is not duly elected" and also "that the said Henry Martin, Esq. (the Bailiff) be for the said offence taken into custody of the Sergeant at Arms attending this House". Later Halsey fought two successful elections and represented in Southwark on and off for about ten years. He followed the practice of other successful citizens of the Borough by acquiring agricultural land and a country seat. He was described in the parish records as "Lord of the Manor" at Stoke Poges where he was buried on his death in 1729. His will assigned not only the property in Southwark but farms at Orpington and Boughton Monchelsea and properties at Newington, Camberwell, Croydon and Mitcham.

The boy Thomas, whose schooling was mentioned in the accounts in 1702, died young as did his brother James. His only daughter, Anne, was successfully married off into the peerage to Richard Temple, Viscount Cobham, friend of Alexander Pope, and creator of the great gardens at Stowe.

When public affairs and his manifold interests were taking up much of his time, Halsey having no sons to follow him, like Child before him brought a young man into the business. This was Ralph Thrale, a Hertfordshire nephew described as "a goodlooking fellow and as industrious as he was comely". This nephew was kept in this place. Dr. Johnson, who later was intimately connected with the Thrales, wrote that this Ralph "worked at six shillings a week for twenty years in the great brewery which afterwards was his own". In fact, Ralph Thrale did not acquire the Anchor Brewery by inheritance. He learnt the business and did very well but managed to put his uncle's nose out of joint domestically. Edmund Halsey's wife had died soon after Ralph's arrival in Southwark. When Ralph took a wife his choice unfortunately fell upon the lady whom his uncle was contemplating as a second Mrs. Halsey. The uncle seems to have accepted the situation without complaint at the time but on his death there was no mention of Ralph in his Will. Lord and Lady Cobham inherited the brewery; failing issue of their marriage the property was to go to Ralph's sister, Anna. Clearly, Ralph Thrale, who had managed the business so successfully, was the only man in a position to continue to run it, and it was agreed that he should pay for it by instalments. The purchase price was £30,000 (a hundred years previously it had changed hands for £400) and it took him eleven years to pay off the money. But if he had not inherited the property he possessed all and more of his uncle's abilities as a brewer and as a public figure. He soon

11. Ralph Thrale who built up the Anchor Brewery at Southwark until his death in 1758 "A good looking fellow and as industrious as he was comely."

12

13

14

12. Henry Thrale, who owned the Anchor Brewery from 1759 to 1781.

13. Mrs. Hester Thrale, Henry's wife and confidante of Dr. Johnson, until her re-marriage to Piozzi.

14. Reynolds portrait of Dr. Samuel Johnson, who played a direct part in the policy and administration of the Anchor Brewery.

15. Birds-eye view of the Southwark Brewery after Barclay Perkins had taken over from Thrale.

16. The Barclay Perkins brewhouse at Southwark in the mid-nineteenth century.

established himself as a man of wealth and influence. He became High Sheriff of Surrey and followed his uncle as M.P. for Southwark. He continued to live in the borough although he and his family frequented fashionable and political circles across the river. His daughter married Sir John Lades who was connected with Thomas Guy, the founder of the hospital. His son Henry went to Eton and Oxford and was encouraged by an allowance of £1,000 a year and Grand Tours in Europe to develop wide interests and liberal tastes. On Ralph Thrale's death in 1758 Henry inherited what was described as "enormous" wealth and Thrale's Brewery. Moreover, he had married one of the most talented, articulate and astonishing women of the century, Hester Salusbury; niece of Sir Thomas Salusbury of Offley, Hertfordshire, the village from which his father Ralph had emerged as a poor relation.

The marriage, the money, the upbringing, political ambitions, and a taste for culture might have combined to induce some men to abandon the brewing of beer in Southwark, however profitable, or to leave it to others. But Henry Thrale stuck to his brewing from the time of his inheritance in 1759 until his death in 1781. In spite of the fact that he was surrounded by the most brilliant company of his time with a wife determined to outshine them all, he followed his father as Sheriff of Surrey and Member for Southwark. He was a conscientious if indifferent brewer and a wildly imprudent man of business. Dr. Samuel Johnson, who became his close friend and sometimes adviser in 1764, and subsequently the dominant figure in Mrs. Thrale's salons, said of him "although in affluent circumstances, he had good sense enough to carry on his father's trade". James Boswell extended the Doctor's quotation: "I remember he once told me he would not quit it for an annuity of ten thousand a year; not, said he, that I get ten thousand a year by it, but it is an estate to my family". At the time of that remark Thrale was brewing some 30,000 barrels of beer annually.

Throughout their reign Henry and Hester Thrale occupied a spacious house within the brewery at Southwark and there, in the course of time, Dr. Johnson had his own quarters and indeed did much of his work, using a chair which is still preserved. The Thrales had a country seat at Streatham which was much preferred to Southwark, but the obligation of maintaining a residence within the confines of the brewery was always observed. Mrs. Thrale, whose writings leave little unrevealed, made this point in recording with her usual candour, the nature of her marriage of convenience to Mr. Thrale (of whom she bore eleven children): "for as I never was a fond Wife, so I certainly never was a Jealous one; I soon saw that I was married from prudential Motives, as a passive, tho' well born & educated Girl; who would be contented to dwell in the Borough, which other Women had refused to do; & my Husband, whose heart was set upon his Business, had it seems always insisted on . . ."

From the time of her marriage at St. Anne's Church, Soho, in 1763 till Henry's death and the subsequent disposal of the brewery in 1781, Hester, while maintaining herself at the height of fashion was dutifully and from time to time deeply involved in the business at Southwark. Being a remarkably articulate writer and an observant, although often prejudiced reporter, she left records of a period of management which was unique in brewing history.

Samuel Johnson became acquainted with the Thrales soon after their marriage. He had a room set aside for him at Streatham as well as at Southwark, and the Thrale household became a second home in which he revelled in unwonted physical comfort and in which his melancholy was eased by the exuberant company of Hester. This remarkable intimacy was not confined to culture; the Doctor became closely and shrewdly connected with the affairs of the brewery.

Early in their acquaintance, according to Mrs. Thrale; "Doctor Samuel Johnson advised me to get a little Book, and write in it all the little Anecdotes which might come to my knowledge . . .". She was 35 years old and had been married thirteen years when Mr. Thrale gave her six handsome blank books bound in calf, each bearing on its cover a red label

stamped in gold with the title 'Thraliana', and it is from the
pages of these journals and from her own pungent footnotes that
we witness much of the intimate life of the Southwark Brewery
in those days.

The Thrales, for instance, in spite of their wealth and
eminence in society, were not at all ashamed of Ralph Thrale's
humble background. On a visit to Hertfordshire they discovered
an old aunt who told the story as it has been outlined in these
pages but enlivened by Hester's pen as she noted it all down in
Thraliana. Her account characteristically winds up with her
own introduction to her future husband: "... hers & her
Brother's Uncle was a Miller's Boy at St. Albans, Edmund
Halsey by Name; that he quarrel'd with his Master the Miller, &
strolled to London, (with 4/6d only in his pocket), where he got
into Child's Brewhouse & worked at their Mill; till by Degrees
he was advanced to places of higher Trust & honor in the
Trade; that he had not been long prefer'd to the Comptinghouse
where he was Clerk, before his Master's only Child & Daughter
cast her Eyes upon him, & in process of Time married him: that
the Father resolving to make the best on't, & finding him useful
in the Business, took him as a Partner, & in time dying left him
& his Wife the Brewhouse – their Inheritance. That Halsey now
at the Head of a prosperous Trade began thinking of his poor
Relations in the Country; more willingly perhaps as his Lady
brought him no Children but a pair of Twins, the eldest of which
dy'd, & the youngest was sought in Marriage for her very great
Fortune by Ld Viscount Cobham who laid out Stowe
Gardens – is celebrated by Mr. Pope &c. and who had by her
no Children at all. Her Father therefore Mr. Halsey sent to
Offley in Hertfordshire, not many miles from St. Albans, to
know what Progeny his *Sister* had, who was married to one
Ralph Thrale a Cottager in that Village of Offley; upon this
Enquiry herself, (who told the Story) & her Brother – *my* Mr.
Thrale's Father – were discovered; She was left behind, but her
Bro^r whose name was Ralph too; was carried to Town to be
made a Man of by his Uncle Edmund Halsey who did not

51

however as I have heard treat him very kindly – tho' he made a Will in his Favour which he afterwards cancelled too, because the poor young Fellow had married a Wench that Halsey wanted to have for his own Pleasure. Notwithstanding all this, and many more Acts of Tyranny – Ralph Thrale, by a Spirit of usefulness & Diligence; and making himself necessary to his Uncle, who found no other Relation he had, half so tractable; got into Lucrative Posts in the Brewhouse, & between borrowing & buying – after Old Halsey's Death obtained Money to purchase, & soon found himself in Possession of the whole: he bought likewise an Estate in Surrey, another in Oxfordshire, provided for his Sister, who told the Story; – & was married to a rich Farmer old Ralph Smith of Saint Albans – and educated his Son & three Daughters quite in a high Style. – The Son he wisely connected with the Cobhams & their Relations – Greenvilles, Lytteltons, & Pitts; to whom he lent Money & they lent Assistance of every kind. – so that *My* Mr. Thrale was bred up at Stowe & Stoke, and Oxford, and every genteel Place; had been abroad with Lord Westcote, whose Expenses of old Thrale chearfully paid I suppose; & who was thus a kind of Tutour to the young Man, who had not failed to profit by these Advantages & who was when he came down to Offley to see his Father's Birthplace, a very handsome and well accomplished Gentleman. – My Mother soon said *this* was the Man for me to *marry,* the only man She said so of; my Uncle in his awkward way said he saw no young Fellow upon the plan of that young Fellow, that he was a *real Sportsman,* and such sort of Stuff; but I soon saw clearly they were both mad for the Match . . ."

Henry Thrale constantly worried over his business, but he gave himself very readily to every kind of diversion. He kept foxhounds, the extravagance of which was criticised by Johnson, and mistresses – the acceptance of which was regarded by Mrs. Thrale with great indulgence. He was involved with a waterworks at Southwark originally planned to supply the Anchor with fresh water but which got into difficulties. He and his wife paid frequent visits to the socially acceptable resorts of Bath, Tunbridge Wells and Brighton. At Streatham there was always lavish entertainment. At Southwark Thrale gave regular dinners on Thursdays. One of his guests has left a note of the Menu: "First course, soups at head and foot, removed by fish and a saddle of mutton: second course, a fowl they called Galena at head, and a capon larger than some of our Irish turkeys at foot: third course, four different sorts of ices, pineapple, grape, and raspberry: and a fourth. In each remove, there were, I think, fourteen dishes, the two first served in massy plate". Then there was a special dinner at the Brewery in May 1773 attended by Sir Joshua Reynolds, Johnson, Goldsmith, Garrick and Burke. The table on this occasion was laid in one of the new brewing coppers and the principal dish was beefsteak dressed at the furnace.

Small wonder that from time to time there were financial crises. 1772 was a particularly bad year. It began serenely enough for Mrs. Thrale: "I was grown fond of my Poultry my Dairy &c. & had now no other Desire than that of sitting down safely & quietly at Streatham to which of late I had rather begun to attach myself". There were clouds, however. First, because her mother seemed to be dying of cancer, then because of the behaviour of Mr. Thrale. Her account of this includes one of her immortal footnotes, here added to the text in brackets:- "Mr. Thrale had for some Time appeared pensive and gloomy – when I asked the Cause, he told me it was something relative to his Business: I grew more inquisitive & he told me that it was the bad Hops he had bought the year before which had spoyl'd all his Beer: I would have laughed at this, but found the Business too serious, and indeed he lost all Sleep & Appetite so fast that it alarmed me; (I was big with Child – as I almost always am. *Mrs. Thrale.*), the more, as Fordyce had lately broke, & cast a Cloud somehow over all the Commercial World. Nesbitt too had I heard been somewhat singed, & I concluded tho' I said nothing – that our Misfortune was of the same kind, however, bad Beer might be the Pretence to *Me*. well but said I methinks if the Beer is really bad, you should send for Jackson to cook it;

he turned from me upon these Words in an Agony I could not then comprehend, but recovered himself so far as to bid me say nothing to my Mother, or to any living Soul of what he had told me. One whole Week I passed therefore in silent Sorrow & Amazement, at the End of which he told us all himself – I mean my Mother & Dr. Johnson, & begged for Counsel & Comfort. We gave him what Counsel & Comfort we could; My Mother said She had 2 or 3 Thousand Pounds at his Service – it was her all, but She could live on her Annuity, which if Things came to the worst we should share with her. If Sir Thos w^d but *dye* She said, as he had no Sons; we should be sure of the Welch Estate, & there was hopes of the Hertfordshire one. Johnson drove me to Town; insisted on my talking to the Clerks authoritatively, & knowing how & why this Calamity had fallen on us: my Mothers Delicacy was blunted about the Trade – and when I came to examine into Things, what was my Astonishment to hear that the Enemy & the Adversary was that wicked *Haman! Jackson* had perswaded my Master to buy the bad Hops, *Jackson* had taught him to brew without Malt; *Jackson* had made him build a Copper to boyl Timber in, at an immense Expense, & all the Timber boil'd in it was rotten. *Jackson* had his Confidence so completly that none of his own Clerks durst speak to him, they therefore resolved to depart. I now tried first to conciliate the necessary People about the Brewhouse, who declared they would not live *with Mr. Thrale,* but they would do *anything* for *me;* only says They Madam get rid of that *Fiend!* he will entirely ruin your whole Family else. I did so, and we soon began to understand each other. Money was raised, the Beer was mended, our whole Conduct in the management of our Trade was changed, and we grew prosperous, and loved each other. – Women have a manifest Advantage over Men in the doing Business; everything smooths down before them, & to be a Female is commonly sufficient to be successful, if She has a little spirit & a little common Sense."

Dr. Johnson, of course, was in the thick of things. He urged economies foreseeing "a year of struggle and difficulty."

Though he was in no way financially involved, he by this time identified himself so completely with the Thrales' interests that he wrote "the first consequence of our late trouble ought to be an endeavour to brew at a cheaper cost ... unless this can be done, nothing can help us." During this crisis the business was in debt to the tune of about £130,000 but by reorganisation, and improved management this deficit was completely cleared in the course of the following nine years.

6

A man who had a great deal to do with this recovery was John Perkins, the Chief Clerk whose name and character emerges for the first time during this period. Perkins was a good man of business, well able to take responsibility in routine matters and, as we shall see, in emergencies, and a man of ambition both financially and socially. He was in the concern in which first the Halseys and the Thrales had arisen from rags to riches. He spent many years of frustration attempting to follow their example. It seems to have been in his character that he never presented the image of a go-getter, but that surrounded by such personalities as Hester and Henry Thrale, Dr. Johnson and the circle of influential friends and advisers, his own personality could never sufficiently establish itself. Clearly during the row over Jackson and the threat of a walk-out by the clerical staff, poor John Perkins felt himself under attack from every quarter. When Mrs. Thrale more or less took charge of affairs he did not hesitate to open his heart to her and, subsequently the running of the business was frequently discussed in confidence between them. Hester recorded a conversation with him in 1773 when he complained "Why 'tis a hard thing Mrs. Thrale (those were his words) to live always in Servitude, a Servitude never made light by kind or even civil Treatment". In the same year he complained to her that Thrale had "not done trying Experiments", as he left a cask of sick beer worth £600 perish when it might have been cured with "50 barrels of good stout porter". At a later stage when Thrale's mind seemed to be disordered, Hester noted "Perkin's Expression was that our Master was Planet-struck".

Whatever the state of his physical and mental health, Henry

Thrale persisted with his brewing and with plans for the development of the business, with John Perkins at his elbow always in a state of anxiety, not without justification. Things frequently went wrong and were recorded by Hester as diligently as were her social triumphs. In 1778 she wrote "Mr. Thrale over brewed himself last Winter, and made an artificial Scarcity of Money in the Family which has extremely lowered his Spirits: Mr. Johnson endeavoured last night & so did I, to make him promise that he would never brew a larger Quantity of Beer in one Winter than eighty Thousand Barrels; but my Master – mad with the noble Ambition of emulating Whitbread & Calvert – two Fellows that he despises – could scarcely be prevailed on to promise even *this,* that he will not brew more than fourscore Thousand Barrels a Year for five Years to come. He did promise *that* much, however; & so Johnson bade me write it down in the Thraliana . . ."

The following year at a time of national crisis when "Publick Concerns now claim every one's Attention", Hester gave vent to an agonised cry. "In the midst of publick & private Distress, here is my mad Master going to build at the boro' House again:- new Store Cellars, Casks, & God knows what. I have, however, exerted myself & driv'n off his Workmen with a high Hand. – Is this a Time as Elijah say'd, for oliveyards, & Vineyards? Men Servants & Maid Servants? when our Trade & our profits are both decreasing daily? & the Nation itself stagnating with Embecillity? I never saw anything so absurd – surely his *head* is *still confused;* nothing but *frenzy* can at this Time excuse Expence to the amount of ten or twelve Thousand Pounds sure".

When the next crisis came to Southwark, the Thrales were away on a round of pleasure at Bath, and John Perkins became the hero of the occasion. In June 1780 the No-Popery riots led by Lord George Gordon broke out and mobs rampaged in London for about a week. Henry Thrale as a public figure had shown some sympathy to the cause of the emancipation of the Roman Catholics. This gave rise to the rumour that Thrale himself was a Papist, and consequently the brewery became a target for violence. The mob came direct from the assault on Newgate Prison and the release of the prisoners for their first attack on the brewery. They carried Newgate chains with them as spoils. John Perkins faced them at the gate. According to the *Gentleman's Magazine* he mildly protested, "it were a shame that men should be degraded by so heavy a load; and he would furnish them with a horse for that purpose". The bait succeeded. He gave them some porter, and they departed with loud Hourahs!" James Boswell amplified the incident, "the brewery was not in great danger, and at the first invasion the rioteers were passive with fifty pounds worth of meat and porter". After this Perkins took no chances; the brewery was manned by troops when the mob made their second attack.

As soon as the Thrales heard the rumour at Bath that they were likely to come under attack they "made a dawdly Journey across the country to Brighton where all was likely to be at peace ..." There Hester learned of Perkins' heroic conduct which was duly rewarded, "Letters ... shewed us how near we were to Ruin here in the Borough; where nothing but the astonishing Presence of Mind shewed by Perkins in amusing the Mob with Meat & Drink & Huzzaes, till Sir Philip Jennings Clarke could get the Troops & pack up the Counting House Bills Bonds &c. & carry them which he did to Chelsea College for Safety; – could have secured us from actual Undoing. The Villains *had* broke in & our Brewhouse would have blazed in ten Minutes; when a property of £150,000 would have been utterly lost, & its once flourishing possessors quite undone.

"Let me stop here, to give God Thanks for so very undeserved, so apparent an Interposition of Providence in our favour.

"I left Mr. Thrale at Brighthelmston, & came to Town again to see what was left to be done: we have now got Arms, & mean to defend ourselves by Force, if further Violence is intended. Whenever I come on these mad Errands, Dear Mr. Johnson is sure always to live with me, & Sir Philip comes every day at some Hour or another:- Good Creature how kind he is! and how much I *ought* to love him! God knows I am not in *this* Case wanting to my Duty. I have presented Perkins by my Master's permission with two hundred Guineas, and a Silver Urn for his *Lady,* with his own Cypher on it . . ."

In fact, Henry Thrale had only authorised the gift of £100 and for some years Hester had to keep quiet about her generosity, but in that same year John Perkins showed that he was not to be satisfied with generous gestures. He had ambitions. In the light of history these seemed justifiable. At the time when they first came into the open, Hester was outraged by them: "Mr. Perkins – the Duce take him – distresses me cruelly: he wants to have a part in the Trade forsooth, & seems to think nothing will pay his Services but that. Mr. Thrale's ill health making His Death too probable, *my* Name may be joined with Perkin's commodiously enough under an Alehouse Checquer. Good God! how such an Idea shocks one! & how little Sensibility has the Proposer of what I am feeling. The Truth is Perkins did behave vastly well both in the dangerous Days of the Year 72. when Mr. Thrale had by implicit Confidence in Jackson reduced his Trade to Distress, and himself to the Necessity of explaining Matters to his Wife, who reconciling Perkins and the rest of 'em, set the Business once more free from the Rock, and heaved her into deep Water – and afterwards in the Year 80. when the Rioters would but for his Skill & attentive Diligence, inevitably have destroyed our whole property – yet I could wish me thinks not to erect a Servant because he is a good Servant, into a Master; and tho' a Man saves my Nation, I see not I, – why he should share my crown. Five hundred a Year I am willing to give the Man, but he has set his Heart upon Power, and tells me – truly enough – that when we first began to understand each other, in the Year 1772, that he swore he never would serve Mr. Thrale, but that he would serve *me,* and abide by my Generosity. – Now I thought my Temper gener-ous enough when I made his Salary – then £300 a Year – £500 a Year by Presents, which I have done ever since, in *hard Money* I mean; besides Presents to his Wife of pieces of Plate &c. He is not satisfied however, & his ill-tim'd urging of his

Claims perplexes me. Mr. Thrale is not in a Situation to be talked to; Johnson & Sr. Philip feel full of Indignation at the Fellow, but that's their Kindness, & not Perkins's Fault – he breaks no point of Compting House Honour, and who should expect a Clerk to behave like a Gentleman? The Man knows he is advancing his Wealth & providing for his Family – what cares he for *my* Anxiety? further than to congratulate himself on being too hard for a Woman of imputed Sense – Duce take him!"

Henry Thrale was indeed suffering from intermittent apoplectic attacks and had only one more year to live, but social life went spinning on. The Thrales reached a new social summit when they took a town house. "So now we are to spend *this* Winter in Grosvenor Square;" wrote Hester in 1781, "My master has taken a ready furnished Lodginghouse there, and we go in tomorrow: He frightened me cruelly a while ago, he would have Lady Shelburne's House – one of the finest in London: he would buy, he would build, he would give 20 30, Guineas a Week for a House? Oh Lord thought I! the people will sure enough throw Stones at me *now,* when they see a Dying Man go to such made Expences, & all – as they will naturally think – to please a Wife wild with the Love of Expence."

Meanwhile, Perkins took up quarters in the brewery. "Perkins takes every step to worm himself into this proposed partnership" Hester wrote, "the artful Creature told Mr. Thrale a Week ago that it was idle of us to be thus at the Mercy of every Brat that could brew – *we have got a young Brewer now:-* that he would himself study the operative part of the Business, & learn the Work done at the Copper Side – how plausible this, & how true? but this Business being almost all Night-Work, he *must* not be deprived of his Wife &c. no sure! so he *must* have an Apartment allotted him in the Dwelling House – Bravo! Mr. Perkins!" To this she appended a footnote: "He wants now to fix himself in the House we are leaving – & tho' I never did anything but wish to leave it Since I lived in it – of Course – yet I hate to be edged out of it by Perkins". However unpalatable the advance of John Perkins might be, it was inevitable that he took more and more control of the business during the last few months of Henry Thrale's life.

He was not named among the executors, who included Dr. Johnson when Thrale died in April 1781, but clearly his value at managerial level was taken for granted. Hester, with her five surviving daughters, inherited the property and the business: "He has been very generous to me in his Will", she wrote, "but my being entangled with the Trade perplexes me greatly – perhaps I may rid my hands of it however, perhaps we may sell it without much Loss: my Coadjutors are all willing to assist while I carry it on, and willing to quit when I wish to part with it: never were Men more obliging to be sure, & I am half inclin'd to hope for Happiness once more, when I see their Disposition to comply with my Desire.

"God forbid though that my Pride or Delicacy should so far influence me as to make me quit the Business *at any Rate:* My Children have a Claim to all that I can do & suffer – yet how will they be benefited by keeping their Money at hazard? Mr. Scrase says 'tis Madness to try at carrying on such a Trade with only five Girls . . . Mr. Johnson did wish my Continuance in Business, but I have pretty well cured him of his Wishes; though when I was obliged Yesterday to go & court a dirty Goaler to suffer our Brewhouse to serve his Tap, & when I complained even with Tears to Mr. Johnson of the Indignity; Dearest Lady says he your Character is exalted by it; I tell you it advances in *Heighth,* Yes replied I, it advances indeed, & *rises* from the *Side* Box to the *upper Gallery.*"

Though she complained greatly, Hester was conscientious, appointing herself to "three Days a Week to attend at the Counting house". No small consolation came from the fact that Dr. Johnson was also involved: "If an Angel from Heaven had told me 20 Years ago, that the Man I knew by the Name of *Dictionary Johnson* should one Day become Partner with me in a great Trade, & that we should jointly or separately sign Notes Draughts &c. for 3 or 4 Thousand Pounds of a Morning, how unlikely it would have seemed ever to happen! – unlikely is no Word tho' – it would have seemed incredible: neither of us then being worth a Groat God knows, & both as immeasurably removed from Commerce, as Birth Literature & Inclination could set us. Johnson however; who desires above all other Good the Accumulation of new Ideas, is but too happy with his present Employment; & the Influence I have over him added to his own solid Judgment and Regard for Truth, will at last find it *in a small degree* difficult to win him from the dirty Delight of seeing his Name in a new Character flaming away at the bottom of Bonds & Leases."

Hester Thrale and the executors soon realised that the business would have to be sold and Hester had purpose to overcome her scruples about the ambitions of John Perkins by offering him a splendid bribe. He was to take over the Thrale dwelling house in the brewery with most of its furniture if he found a purchaser – and with surprising alacrity Perkins came into his own.

An enviable aspect of Hester Thrale's character was her ability to find pleasure in higher things even in the midst of disturbing material situations. She was well aware of this quality in herself. Thus, on May 17th 1781, only a month after her husband's death, she declared: "The power of emptying one's head of a great Thing, and filling it with little ones to amuse Care, is no small Power; & I am proud of being able to write Italian Verses while I am bargaining for £150,000 – & settling an Event of the highest Consequence to my own and my Children's Welfare. David Barclay the rich Quaker will treat for our Brewhouse, & the Negotiation is already begun. My heart palpitates with hope & fear, my Head is bursting with Anxiety & Calculation; yet I can listen to a Singer and translate Verses about a Knife."

The business and social life of London in the eighteenth century always seems by our standards to have proceeded at a leisurely pace. Hester Thrale's circle was quick-witted by any standards in their talks and could be sudden in their amusements, but their movements across the crowded Thames bridges, through the narrow cobbled streets and out into the countryside of winding dusty lanes were indeed sluggish. Their affairs were conducted in chilly, dimly lit counting houses, coffee shops and inns, recorded by the scratch of quill pens with sand to dry the ink, with communication by messenger, carrier or coach with no more despatch than by those of the ancient Romans. So it is a matter of astonishment that the sale of the Anchor Brewery in spite of its attendant anxieties and complaints, took place with a speed which could not be equalled today. Henry Thrale had been dead for less than a month when the executors agreed with Hester to put the business on the market and advertise it for sale by auction. Notices immediately went up on the brewery walls, and it was these which were observed by David Barclay, and by the end of May some six weeks after Thrale's death, a Barclay had joined forces with John Perkins in taking over the business.

It was said that David Barclay, accompanied by Silvanus Bevan, both partners in Barclays Bank, spotted the sale notices while walking across one of the Thames bridges, and said "This business will do for young Robert". This Robert, born in America and sent back to make his way in the business world of London under the powerful guidance of the family, was David Barclay's nephew. David Barclay himself was the grandson of the famous Robert Barclay who wrote the *Apology for the people called in scorn Quakers"* and his family, like that of John Courage, came from Aberdeen where the apologist had, "clothed in sackcloth and ashes, walked through the streets and testified against its people".

With David Barclay and Silvanus Bevan young Robert made a close inspection of the Thrale concern which included the brewhouse, public houses, plant and machinery, and stock-in-trade. The shrewd Quakers were impressed with the managing abilities of John Perkins but dismayed by the way Thrale had conducted the business, by his extravagant way of living and by the unprofitable wildcat schemes on which he squandered his money – one of them the invention of an anti-fouling compound for preserving ships' bottoms.

On the day of the sale, May 31st 1781, there was considerable public interest, for this was no ordinary brewery, but Barclay was the only one who meant business. Hester Thrale went to Southwark early that day. "She told me", wrote Fanny Burney, "that if all went well she would wave a white pocket handkerchief out of the coach window". It is not clear from this where the members of the circle – of which Fanny was one of the most famous – positioned themselves on that day. The successful bid was £135,000, a very substantial sum in those days, to be spread over four years. That it was value for money we are left to no doubt, for Dr. Johnson, in the course of the transaction, stated: "Sir, we are not here to sell a parcel of boilers and vats, but the potentiality of growing rich beyond the dreams of avarice." John Perkins was now rewarded for all that he had suffered in patience. Not only did he get the Thrale house but a partnership in the business. Although Robert Barclay's name was given as the sole purchaser in the documents which bear Dr. Johnson's signature as a witness, there already existed an agreement under which David Barclay, Robert Barclay, Silvanus Bevan and John Perkins should each find one quarter of the price and be equal partners.

Perkins did not find his share of the money too easy; but finally his love-hate relationship with Hester Thrale bore its last somewhat bitter fruit: "We have had another hot storming Day last Tuesday 3rd July" she wrote "about this everlasting Brew house, but 'tis over. Perkins wanted more Indulgence than we as Executors could give him, so I lent him the Money I had saved & put in the Stocks – £2,000 it was, & sold out for £1,600 & odd. He is, or ought to be much obliged; but when a Man has not all he wanted, nothing will make him quite happy. The whole is quite finished, & within three Months too."

So within those three hectic months the scene at the Anchor Brewhouse was transformed. Hester went off to marry her daughter's music teacher Gabriel Piozzi (whom Perkins called

'Powzy' through ignorance or perhaps contempt) at Southwark. For the four years during which the purchase money was being paid the business was carried on under the style of H. Thrale & Company. Thereafter it was changed to Barclay, Perkins & Co. and to this day there are Barclays, Perkins and Bevans with the descendants of John Courage at the head of affairs.

7

Under the new partnership the Anchor lost some of its glamour. Although it remained one of the industrial sights of London for foreign visitors (some seventy years later, in the year of the Great Exhibition, more than 50,000 visitors came to the brewery in the course of five months). Its gain was in efficiency and expansion. This was reflected in the official records as "The Quantity of Beer Brewed by the London Brewers –

1776	Leading Brewers	Whitbread	102,505	barrels
	„	Thrale	75,354	„
1781	„	Whitbread	115,033	„
	„	Barclay, Perkins	80,053	„
1802	„	Meux	143,946	„
	„	Barclay, Perkins	137,405	„
1809	„	Barclay, Perkins	205,328	„
	„	Meux	150,105	„

The industrial acreage at Southwark was increased and, influenced by the Barclay and Bevan family connections with East Anglia, agricultural land and maltings were acquired. Although all the traditions of Southwark brewing were cherished and enhanced, the new people were quick to take advantage of new invention. Steam was coming in to change the industrial face of Britain. Robert Barclay turned his attention to it immediately he arrived in Southwark. Three years later the famous pioneers Boulton and Watt were installing the first steam engine in the brewery. The work was supervised by William Murdock on the instructions of James Watt. The steam power to be used was for raising water from the brewery wells which had been done by a pump powered by horses drawn round a circular track. The "horse-wheel" was a familar feature of breweries of the period and drawings of that at the Anchor have been preserved. Murdock calculated that the average horse worked at the rate of 22,000 feet pounds per minute. He added 50 per cent to this estimate and thus produced the figure of 33,000 feet pounds per minute which thereafter became the established definition of one horsepower. Thus, the Anchor Brewery, already rich in literary associations, added to the lore of engineering. The result of Murdock's work was a steam engine which continued to operate in the brewery for a hundred years, being replaced in 1884 by another engine made by James Watt & Co. described by a contemporary writer as "one of the finest engines in London, which is the admiration of very many visitors in the trade".

In 1810 a foreign visitor, Louis Simond, described the Anchor: "About 200 men are employed; the stock of liquor is valued at £300,000; the barrels alone used to convey the beer to the customers cost about £80,000; the whole capital amounts to not less than half a million. There is stabling for 100 horses - - large fine beasts, capable of much work."

Throughout the eighteenth and nineteenth centuries, South-wark was notorious for its conflagrations. These were due to the intense industrialisation of the area, the inflammatory nature of so much of the merchandise handled on the wharves and the fire risk of the densely-housed population. The frequency and the gravity of these fires were encouraged by lack of safety regulations, but they also encouraged by sheer necessity the development of a fire service in London. The Anchor was a victim in 1832 and the event was reported in The Examiner: "Shortly after 5 o'clock on Tuesday afternoon a fire broke out in the extensive premises of Messrs. Barclay, Perkins & Co. It spread devastation and caused much alarm in the surrounding district ... the fire commenced in an inner quadrangle ... and the flames rapidly spread ... to a distance of 250 feet.

"Information of the fire had been forwarded to Mr. Barclay,

who was attending his Parliamentary duties (Charles Barclay was M.P. for Southwark and subsequently for West Surrey) and that gentleman came on the spot as speedily as possible and gave directions ... One of the squares, containing upwards of 1,000 barrels of beer, burst unexpectedly on a number of firemen ... and the premises were nearly flooded with beer. The total amount of damage, in buildings, machinery, etc., is estimated at £40,000. Messrs. Barclay, Perkins & Co., have another brewery establishment in full operation in Stoney Lane, which, together with the whole of the stock of beer uninjured in Park Street, will enable them to supply their customers as usual."

Another contemporary report stated that when the beams in the malt lofts caught fire, "Mr. John Braithwaite, with a gallon of water under his arm, and two pint-pots in his hands, extinguished these early flames, and so kept the fire in check until more efficient help could be brought." This no doubt refers to James Braithwaite, the pioneer of steam fire-engines, who had been promoting his elegant carriage-like land steamer during this period. Although he had failed to interest the great James Braidwood in his invention, one of his machines assisted in controlling the fire. Afterwards – by what financial arrangement is not recorded – it stayed on at the Anchor in service as a beer-pump until new equipment was organised. Perhaps as a result of the fire, Robert Barclay later diversified his interests by joining the Court of the Royal Exchange.

The business itself ultimately benefited from the fire. The Insurance Cyclopaedia written some years later by Cornelius Walford presented a flourishing picture: "Thanks to the good fortune which in days when the clay of London had not yet become far more valuable per square foot than the goldmines of Russian and Brazil – Australia and California were not yet thought of – gave them so extensive an area on which to erect all necessary buildings, Barclay and Perkins, unlike some of their largest rivals, are enabled to be their own maltsters. How great an advantage this is, only a brewer knows; and the malthouses in Park Street are indeed sights to see, and to be followed, from the cranes by which the barley is hoisted from waggons into the buildings, past the screens where it is cleansed, the cisterns where it is steeped, the couching frames where it is gauged by the exciseman, and the floors where the process of germination is perfected, to the kilns where it is roasted until it receives the required colour, and so on to the bins where it is stored until wanted to be made into beer."

The rebuilt Anchor of Victorian times was a proud institution. In the visitors' book the signatures included Prince Albert, the Prince of Wales, Napoleon III, the Emperor of Russia, Prince Osman Pacha, Comte de Paris, Garibaldi and Don Carlos. Such visitors admired not only the brewing of the beer but the splendours of the horses and indeed of the men. Alfred Barnard, writing in the eighteen-eighties, said: "As is well-known the draymen in Barclay's wear the Phrygian red cap of liberty, and are supplied by the firm with long white overalls and deep leather collars giving them a picturesque appearance. All are picked men of great stature and strength, who move the great butts and barrels about as if they were toys. There are more than fifty of these handsome fellows, who take great pride in their teams, and are scrupulous as to the appearance of the harness and general turn-out."

Another witness writing about the same time was Dr. William Rendle, who said "The draymen and the horses at Barclay's were, and I suppose are, fine specimens of their kind; the horses were wonders in size and appearance. The draymen some less. I attended many of them, notably one gigantic man, for erysipelas, and as it was needful I should know, so as to guide my treatment, how much he took daily, I asked him. 'Why, you see, sir,' said he, 'that I am one of the oldest of the men who go with the drays, and so my journeys are the short ones. I get a little drink at each place (besides what we get at the brewery) – beer and a drop of gin or what not.' – 'How much altogether?' I asked. 'About three gallons then besides.' I could scarcely see how he managed to take it all down, but that was what he said. My practical conclusion was, 'Well, to get you over the erysipelas you must go on much the same.' He recovered. I must say the men, so far as the shell was concerned, were often as fine as the horses, but there was a dreamy muddled look about the eyes, and they had a shambling sort of walk. This was many years ago; I practised in Southwark nearly fifty years."

Whether they succumbed to their temptations or not, the brewery people at all levels maintained a sturdy independence of character. There was, for instance, a building within the precincts of the brewery which had lingered on from the Thrales' time and was noticed by Alfred Barnard: ". . . for here it is that the *twelve apostles* make their appearance on the first Thursday afternoon in every month, precisely as the clock strikes four. Start not, gentle reader, at the assertion; they are not *Heavenly visitants* appearing at stated times to assist in the beneficent labours of John Barleycorn 'within the precincts,' but in reality twelve genial souls, who have succeeded their fathers in the 'Apostolate,' and every one of them labourers in the great work of supplying thirsty Britons with Barclay's life-giving product; a chosen few of the brewery disciples who meet to celebrate each other's birthday in toast and speech. The position of President, which is an honourable one, is permanent, and the duties are carried out with great strictness and ceremony. Each apostle in turn treats his brethren to a bottle of vintage claret and two of old port, no white wines being allowed under any circumstance. All the members of this conclave are either managers of departments or chief clerks in the brewery, and several of these gentlemen, to whom we were introduced, concealed under a grave demeanour much fun and humour. On certain occasion, during the assembling of the *saints,* one of these cheerful spirits was summoned on a matter of business to the presence of a member of the firm, who had either forgotten this 'assemblage of the saints', or did not know of its existence. Enquiring the reason of so long a delay in answering the message, the gentleman replied with perfect simplicity, 'why sir, it was impossible for me to attend earlier, this is Thursday afternoon and I am one of the apostles,' to which Mr. Perkins (for he it was) replied, 'is that so; and are you the Judas Iscariot of the assembly?'"

The forthrightness of brewery people in particular and of Southwark people in general led to an incident at the Anchor during Queen Victoria's reign which had international repercussions. A certain Baron Julius Jacob Von Haynau arrived in this country in 1850. An Austrian by birth, he had risen to high rank in the Hapsburg army. In Italy he had been in charge of repressing revolt and he carried out his duties so brutally at Brescia that he had become known as the 'Hyaena of Brescia'. Afterwards he had become dictator of Hungary where his hangings and floggings were even more notorious. His evil reputation had spread throughout Europe when arrived in Britain shortly after his deposition in Hungary. The reason for his visit to a relatively liberal-minded country where he was unlikely to be welcomed is unknown; although it is known at least that Lord Palmerston then Foreign Secretary, was critical of his presence.

Haynau went the rounds of a distinguished foreign visitor and in due course arrived in Southwark and signed his name in the visitors' book at the Anchor, prior to viewing the wonders of the brewery in all its mid-Victorian splendour. But before the ink of his signature was dry, the office clerks were spreading the news of his arrival, shouting "Down with the Austrian butcher."

Accounts of what happened vary, but of the severity of the near-lynching there is no doubt. It began in the brewery by somebody dropping a truss of hay on the visitor's head. Then he was surrounded, pelted and abused by the brewery people who were joined by men and women from the market as he tried to make his escape. Because so many of his own atrocities had been against women, the women of Southwark were particularly ferocious. Haynau fled along Bankside and took refuge in the George public house where, according to some accounts, he was hidden in a dustbin. His life was saved by the multitudinous doors and devious passages of the old inn, which confused his pursuers. Fortunately for him a police rowing galley was alongside and the police managed to rush him on board and row him across the river to safety. "He escaped with his life and lost his moustache" wrote one of the newspapers, referring to his enormous military moustache which had found much favour with characterists. Newspapers and journals, particularly 'Punch,' took up the incident with relish, and the Barclay, Perkins draymen were the heroes of the hour. The incident, however, did not close with the newspapers' stories and the retreat of Haynau across the Channel (he died aged 67 in bed in Vienna three years later).

The Austrian Ambassador demanded formal apologies from the British Government. Palmerston's sympathies were clearly with the draymen. His own view was that the "Ferocious and unmanly treatment of the unfortunate inhabitants of Brescia and of other towns and places in Italy, his savage proclamations to the people of Pesth and his barbarous acts in Hungary excited almost as much disgust in Austria as in England." Accordingly he first delayed answering the Ambassador and then sent off a letter without waiting for Queen Victoria's approval of its contents. On receiving the draft, the Queen disapproved very strongly. Palmerston had to defend himself with a note to the Queen: "Viscount Palmerston had put the last paragraph into the answer because he could scarcely have reconciled it to his own feelings and to his sense of public responsibility to have put his name to a note which might be liable to be called for by Parliament, without expressing in it, at least as his personal opinion, a sense of the want of propriety evinced by General Haynau in coming to England at the present moment . . . The state of public feeling in this country about General Haynau and his proceedings in Italy and Hungary was perfectly well known . . . the brewers' men were expressing their feelings at what they considered inhuman conduct on the part of General Haynau . . . who was looked upon as a great moral criminal." The Queen's irritation was not assuaged. She forwarded Palmerston's note to the Prime Minister, Lord John Russell: "Lord John will see that Lord Palmerston has not only sent the draft, but passes over in silence her injunction to have a corrected copy given to Baron Keller (The Ambassador), and adds a vituperation against General Haynau which clearly shows that he is not sorry for what has happened, and makes a merit of sympathising with the draymen at the brewery."

The immediate outcome was that Palmerston, having threatened to resign, had to withdraw the message he had sent to Vienna, and a more apologetic note took its place. But the effect of the draymen's action lingered on. The Austrians refused to send an official representative to the funeral of the Duke of Wellington two years later in 1852, and by this time the Queen's views on the incident were more liberal. She expressed surprise that Austria should "slight England in return for what happened to Haynau for his own character."

Public opinion, however, was strongly in sympathy with the Southwark protest. Broadsides and street ballads for many years acclaimed the actions of the draymen. In September 1850 there was even a public meeting at Farringdon Hall in which their "noble conduct" was approved and cheered. When the Italian hero Garibaldi came to London fourteen years later in 1864, one of his most popular gestures was to insist on seeing the "fabrique de biere" where the tyrannical Haynau had been humilated. At the Anchor Garibaldi toasted the workmen of the world in good Southwark Beer.

One of the partners who welcomed Garibaldi was Henry, son (or grandson) of John Perkins (Hester, long after her retirement from the scene, quotes a Dr. Parr as saying "the young Perkinses were sad mean Boys, I sent them as Students to him at their Mother's request who fancied they would be Scholars: but they prov'd poor Creatures it seems – No Wonder! . . .")

Nevertheless, the Perkins family kept a literary tradition alive at the Anchor. Henry Perkins, conscious of historic associations, became a great book collector and possessed four folio editions of Shakespeare. When his library was auctioned in 1873 it realised the then enormous sum of over £26,000.

Family tradition and succession was cherished at Bankside as it was with the Courages at Horselydown. Even in the eighteen-seventies when family businesses were more the rule than the exception, Barnard was impressed: "Messrs. Barclay's is entirely a family business, unique of its kind in the kingdom, the founders having carefully limited it, even to the order of names in the deeds. The present partners are Robert, Charles Arthur, Thomas George, Hedworth Trelawney (the owner of the world-renowned race horse, 'Bendigo,' for which a sum of £10,000 has been refused), Alexander Charles Barclay, Colonel R. S. Paley, J. Bagot Scriven, Augustus F. Perkins, A. E. Perkins, Alfred H. Bevan and Frederick L. Bevan." It is no surprise to find the surnames repeated in 1896 when Barclay, Perkins & Co. became a public company with Robert Barclay as Chairman.

Exactly one hundred years before that event Farrington was writing in his diary "I drank some Porter Mr. Lindoe had from Thrale's Brewhouse. He said it was specially brewed for the Empress of Russia and would keep seven years." This is one of several references to export trade which was built up by the brewers of Southwark, extending to Europe, to the New World and to the Far East. The most notable of these exports taken over from the days of Thrale was undoubtedly Barclay's Imperial Russian Stout. While it still bore the Thrale label in 1795, the author of "The History and Antiquities of the Parish of St. Saviour, Southwark," extolled it: "The reputation and enjoyment of Porter is by no means confined to England. As a proof of the truth of this assertion, this house exports annually very large quantities; so far extended are its commercial connections that Thrale's intire is well known, as a delicious beverage, from the frozen regions of Russia to the burning sands of Bengal and Sumatra. The Empress of all Russia is, indeed so partial to Porter, that she has ordered repeatedly very large quantities for her own drinking and that of her Court.

It refreshes the brave soldiers who are fighting the battles of their country in Germany and animates with new ardour and activity the colonists of Sierra Leone and Botany Bay. It is not only evident from the exportation of other articles, but likewise from the quantity of Porter sent abroad, that Thrale's intire extends the reputation of British produce to the inmost quarters of the Globe."

References to "intire" or "entire" in descriptions of brewery products in earlier times – and these words still sometimes appear – have often mystified laymen. After visiting the sign-writing department at the Anchor in the eighteen-eighties, Barnard offered this explanation: "Being much puzzled as to the meaning of the word 'Entire', we were obliged to enquire of our guide, who soon made it plain to us. He stated that in by-gone days beer retailers were wont to sell a kind of liquor called 'half-and-half', that is half ale and half twopenny, which had to be drawn from two casks; afterwards a taste was gradually acquired for 'three-thread', a compound of ale, beer, and twopenny, which the retailer was necessitated to draw from three casks; a process so troublesome, that it led to the brewing of a kind of beer which should combine the qualities of the three sorts, and which, being drawn from one cask, obtained the name of 'entire butt beer'. It seems strange, that now the circumstances under which the necessity arose have long since passed away that the term should remain, and still be retained on the boards."

The merchant shipping of the Thames tideway had played an important part in the background at Bankside as in the Courage business at Horselydown. Child, the man who gave the Anchor its name, had been closely connected with the supply of beer to the navy. Wherever the navy sailed in the eighteenth and early nineteenth centuries it carried its own supplies of beer, and during the expansionist period of British history, beer followed the flag. Markets were opened in Africa, Asia, India, America and the West Indies.

The European trade, in which such products as Barclay's

Russian Stout was prominently featured, was the result of commercial expediency and its origins go further back. The demands of industry, then mainly in the south of England during the sixteenth century caused wide-spread stripping of forests and woodland. It became necessary to import timber for ship-building as a matter of national security. This timber came from Northern Europe and the brewers needed it for their casks as urgently as the ship-builders for their hulks. Beer was exported to balance the import of timber, and as early as 1591 Stow mentions the export of 26,400 barrels of beer "from twenty great brewhouses on Thames side from Milford Stairs in Fleet Street to below St. Catherine's.

Thus, the Baltic, Russian and the German markets for Southwark beer which flourished in the nineteenth century were based on long tradition. The demand for the timber for casks was enormous. Cornelius Walford, visiting the Anchor in late Victorian times – and there was much expansion to come – – marvelled at the figure of a half a million barrels which passed through the cooperage department: "All these are made, re-paired, cleaned, and examined in the yard, under competent superintendence. It is difficult to realise what half a million barrels really mean, so, by way of illustration, let us say that if placed side by side, bilge to bilge, they would extend from the brewery to Dover, thence to Deal, and back again to Park Street, and then leave enough to surround London with a strong rampart of beer."

The traditional trade with Russia vanished with the First World War, and that with the Baltic and Northern Europe has diminished during the last few decades. But, as we shall see, the world-wide export and manufacture has more than filled its place and timber is no longer required for brewers' casks any more than it is needed for the hulls of ships.

During the present century up to the First World War, Barclay Perkins, like many others, went through a thin time and, for some years at least, no dividends were paid. After the war, however, they followed the expansionist trend of all the great breweries and their special triumph was the pioneering of Barclays' Lager both in Britain and with a large overseas trade and the slogan "An Empire Drink For An Empire Thirst". In 1929 they took over Style & Winch Ltd., the Dartford Brewery Co., and The Royal Brewery, Brentford, Ltd. The Brentford Brewery had a distinguished ancestry in the person of Sir Felix Booth, Bart., 1775-1850, who was a distiller as well as a brewer, a Sheriff of London and Middlesex, and was deeply interested in polar expeditions. He financed Capt. Ross's "Voyage of Discovery" in 1828 to explore the Polar Seas. It was this expedition which discovered the Magnetic Pole in 1831.

In recognition of Booth's services, William IV bestowed the Royal Coat of Arms upon the brewery at Brentford, and with the merging of the concerns the royal privilege was transferred to Southwark. A feature of this particular distinction, shared only with the Dome at Brighton, is that the grant is in perpetuity and need not be renewed upon the death of a reigning sovereign.

The Style & Winch marriage followed a long commercial flirtation for Barclay, Perkins & Co. had been associated with the Medway Brewery for many years. Style & Winch had been built up through a series of such marriages and amalgamations over the course of a century involving over twenty breweries and cider makers, and their business extended from Kent and East Sussex over the South East and into London. They also possessed their own hopfields and mineral factory. The first Medway Brewery was built by William Baldwin in 1806 at the time when the five-arch road-bridge was rebuilt at Maidstone. A John Holme joined the partnership and in the eighteen-fifties the firm traded as Baldwin & Holmes, and in the sixties as Holmes & Style. When the South Eastern Railway (Strood to Maidstone) was promoted in 1853, the line cut off the springs supplying the brewery and the Act of Parliament authorising this laid down that the railway company should pump for the brewery "good and wholesome water equal in quantity and quality to . . . the water diverted."

In 1886 H. W. Tyrwhitt-Drake joined the brewery. His son,

Sir Garrard Tyrwhitt-Drake, in this century became Deputy Chairman of the Company and one of the best known of Medway citizens, and the family zoo and circus was a popular attraction at Cobtree Manor, said to have been the inspiration for Charles Dickens' Dingley Dell. In Victorian times, with the population of Maidstone more than doubling itself, the business prospered. Inevitably – the calamity so often seems to repeat itself – there was a serious fire in the eighteen-nineties and afterwards much rebuilding. By the end of the century the buildings and plant had been modernised and the firm, then known as A. F. Style & Co., amalgamated with E. Winch & Sons, Ltd., of Chatham. So Style & Winch entered the present century with a strong well integrated territory.

For a concern which seems in every other respect to have been progressive, it is curious to note that the new Board of Directors put their names to a petition against the installation of electric light in Maidstone. In 1902, however, they were purchasing their first steam wagon capable of speeds between four and five miles per hour.

After Style & Winch took over the Brentford brewery, all beer was brewed at Maidstone and carried up to the London tideway from the Medway in the firm's own sailing barges, and these shipments continued until the nineteen-thirties. Until the late forties power-driven barges carried Style & Winch beer from Maidstone to Rochester for distribution in the Medway towns. One of the last uses of water transport was for the conveyance of Barclays' stout from the Thames tideway to Scotland.

During the nineteenth century both Style and Winch houses had sold Barclay's Stout. In many old photographs of inn signs Barclay's name appears beside that of one of the Medway brewers, and thus collaboration continued throughout the early part of the century. Before the First World War, Style & Winch bought up Vallance's of Sittingbourne, Simmonds of Hadlow, the Ashford Breweries, and the Lion Brewery in Chatham. In 1924 they acquired the Dartford Brewery, which had been established in 1800 and had acquired concerns at Tonbridge, Dartford and Northfleet. In 1929 Major C. A. C. Perkins was among the Directors from the Anchor who joined the Maidstone Board, while representatives of both the Style and Winch families joined the Board of Barclay, Perkins in London.

A major overseas enterprise of the fifties was the establishment of The Blue Nile Brewery at Khartoum in the Republic of Sudan. This was the first brewery to be started in that country and the first to be planned and built overseas by any of the companies destined to form the Courage Group.

The idea of building a brewery in the Anglo-Egyptian Sudan (as it then was) came from the late John Loughnan, Export Manager of Barclay Perkins & Co., who first put it to his Board in 1950. After much hesitation, due largely to the uncertainties of Middle East politics, at a time when the Sudan's progress towards independence hung in the balance, the decision to go ahead was taken and work on the construction of the brewery started in September, 1953. The first trial brew was put through in July, 1955 and beer was put on the market on 14th December of that year, just over a fortnight before the country became independent – a coincidence which was duly emphasised in the company's first publicity.

The brewery stands on part of a fine 26-acre site, leased from the Sudan Government and was originally designed for an output of 25,000 barrels a year – a total which has since been exceeded, when sales have been buoyant, as a result of the installation of more modern plant in the bottling hall.

The company is registered in the Sudan and there are some substantial local shareholders; but two thirds of the capital was provided by Barclay Perkins & Co., so that the Courage Group now holds a controlling interest.

The brewer's staff and employees are nearly all Sudanese and there have never been more than five "expatriates" in charge. During the sixties there were only four – the Managing Director, the Head Brewer and his Assistant and the Accountant. The Company Secretary is a Sudanese, who was the first member of the staff to be recruited locally, in the very early days of the construction period.

Apart from very small quantities of stout and brown ale (known locally as "dark beer"), the brewery concentrates entirely on the production of lager beer of the continental type, modelled on the Dutch and German lagers which had captured the greater part of the local market – and created the local taste – in the years immediately after World War II.

The beer was an immediate success and was virtually the first industrial product of the Sudan to achieve a quality closely comparable with that of the imported article. In the early years, the problem was not selling the beer, but producing enough to satisfy the claimant demand and in subsequent years sales have only varied with the ups and downs of the Sudanese economy and politics: when times have been good, the brewery has always had to work to capacity and "Camel Beer" – so called from the Company's well-known camel trade mark – has become an accepted feature of Sudanese life.

Simultaneously, with the brewing of the Sudanese beer came the merger of Barclay, Perkins with Courage. By the time they joined forces with their Bermondsey neighbour in 1955, the Barclay, Perkins concern had undergone a massive twentieth century expansion in cider, lager, in export business, and in public houses throughout greater London, Essex, Kent and Sussex. The combined forces of the two concerns controlled some 2,500 tiedhouses as well as extensive free trade interests. The merger had a curious personality of its own in that the Courages, and the Barclays, Bevans, and Perkins were still represented by individuals in the Board Room. They were shortly to be joined by another family name already renowned in brewing – that of Simonds.

17. Simonds Shop at
30 Queen Street, Oxford.
Already there were
Simonds connections at big
British garrison towns at
home and overseas.

18. The great red lion in
Forbury Gardens Reading,
sculptured by George
Blackall Simonds as a
Memorial to the Berkshire
men who fell in the Afghan
War of 1880.

19

20

21

Sir

Reading 15 June 1814

I have taken the liberty to address you
respecting the supply of your Canteen at
Sandhurst with Beer — Having supplied the
College for some time past I beg leave to
refer you to the Commanding Officers of the
same for the Satisfaction I have given
should you have it in your Power to
assist me I shall esteem it a particular
favor —

I am Sir
with the due respects
of — Obt Hble Servt
Wm B Simonds

22. George Blackall Simonds 1843/1929. Sculptor and falconer. Chairman of Simonds Brewery.

SIMONDS

8

From the Southwark tideway some forty miles upstream at Reading, the House of Simonds was founded in 1785, just two years before John Courage went into brewing. The Simonds' roots were deeply set in the countryside in contrast to those of Courage, Barclay and Perkins which were entirely urban. But these contrasting origins in fact followed the progressive pattern of the brewing industry as it emerged from the eighteenth century. The brewers of Southwark, essentially metropolitan in outlook, gradually spread their interests out towards the countryside from which they drew their natural resources. Such brewers as Simonds started by serving a rural community and worked towards a more sophisticated urban industrial form. Owing to its geographical situation, which brought it into contact with Victorian military life, the Simonds concern developed a unique overseas trade with establishments at such outposts as Gibraltar, Malta and Cyprus.

But apart from this important development, which took place when the firm was already well established, the Simonds story offers a classic example, repeated all over the country, of the integration of brewing with farming and agricultural finance. The growing connections between brewing and banking in the eighteenth century have been noted by Peter Mathias " . . . men who had become personally wealthy in banking brought that wealth, and their banking associations into the partnerships of breweries. The families of Barclay, Bevan, Gurney, Hanbury, Brown, Hobhouse, Hoare, Wilshere, Clutterbuck, are examples of this movement . . . On the brewers' side the need was clear enough, but there was a mingling of motives on the part of the banking families who accepted the new associations. Often, established bankers would put a son or relative into brewing, rather than become involved himself (as with Robert Barclay or George M. Hoare or Sampson Hanbury). In this case, there need be no more economic significance in the move than the fact that brewing was a highly prosperous and secure occupation in which a young man with capital might invest his money and energy with advantage."

The Simonds family was characteristic. William Blackall Simonds, who founded the brewery, came from a family which had prospered in Berkshire since Saxon times. They had been farmers, millers, maltsters, lawyers and landowners. With a background of such interests it was natural that in the eighteenth century some of them should have established themselves as bankers, and it was with existing family connections with banking that William Blackall Simonds founded his brewery in 1785. Some five years later he entered into a partnership which became known as J. & C. Simonds, Bank of Reading, which flourished in Berkshire until 1913 when it was absorbed by Barclays. At the time of this amalgamation the Reading Bank had twelve branches.

At one period the bank and the brewery occupied the same premises, but in other respects their identities and their management remained separate. After going into brewing, however, William Blackall Simonds retained many financial interests. He was Town Treasurer for Reading in 1793, 1802 and 1817, and he was also Receiver General of Taxes for Berkshire. Like the Southwark brewers, the Simonds dynasty was much concerned with public affairs. During the course of the years they gave the nation a Lord Chancellor, Berkshire two High Sheriffs and Reading five Mayors.

Besides his banking connections and his established position, William Blackall Simonds was fortunate in possessing some property which was to have geographical significance to the brewing business in after years. In his grandfather's Will dated 1765 he received "all my Farm and Lands in the Parish of Sandhurst lately in the occupation of Thomas Sandford." Thus he was already a landowner at Sandhurst when the Royal Military College opened there in 1813. Local geography, the lie of the land and rural habits in fact play a very potent part in the Simonds development.

There were already five breweries in Reading when Simonds opened in Broad Street in 1785. It was a small local trade but it prospered sufficiently for him to move to the site in Bridge Street on the West bank of the River Kennet where the business has remained. This riverside situation was to be of great importance for the next century or more because of the vital part water-transport played in brewing, even after the development of the railways. The brewery possessed splendid artesian wells which still exist, and there was no question of the site having been chosen in order to turn the Kennet water into beer. The position rather afforded a focal point for the network of interests which was to grow with the brewery during the nineteenth century. The present pattern of railways, in which Reading is so well placed, had already been in existence for nearly half a century (William's son Henry Simonds was one of the original directors and later Deputy Chairman of the Great Western Railway which came to Reading in 1840) when Barnard wrote in 1891: "The Kennet falls into the Thames about half a mile from the brewery, whence it is navigable for barges of 110 tons as far as Newbury, and joining the Kennet and Avon Canal affords communication with Bath, Bristol and the Severn. The Thames affords means of transport to the Metropolis for articles of bulk, and it is by this route that Messrs. H. & G. Simonds frequently send beer to their London stores at Millbank Wharf."

From the start the structure of the business remained a family concern. After the turn of the century the founder's two sons, Henry and George, were taken into the business. But the main succession passed to his three sons, Blackall (1784-1875), Henry (1785-1874) and George (1794-1852). Of these, Henry continued to pursue his own business as a vintner until his wine and spirit business was merged with the brewery in 1868.

It was William's first son, Blackall, who was most active in promoting the brewery development. His most successful achievement arose from a remarkable capacity for combining business with pleasure.

He was an enthusiastic follower of hounds and it was in the hunting fields that he first got wind of impending legislation which was to alter the whole pattern of the brewing industry. The Duke of Wellington was Prime Minister when, in 1830, the Chancellor of the Exchequer announced the abolition of the beer tax. New legislation known as the Duke of Wellington's Beer Act not only removed the duty on beer but it gave anyone the right to retail beer by paying an annual licence of two guineas. Thus a new area of trade was intentionally opened up, one of the objects being to discourage the formidable consumption of spirits which had more than doubled during the first three decades of the nineteenth century. The Act stated that the newly created beer houses were not to open before 4.00 a.m. and were to close down by 10.00 p.m.

Having been tipped off about the government's intention Blackall Simonds foresaw the impact of the new legislation upon his own immediate surroundings. So while he continued to hunt the countryside within fifteen miles of Reading, he carefully noted down suitable sites for public houses to enjoy the benefit of the new retail trade as soon as the Duke of Wellington's Act was passed. He was assisted by a sagacious groom, whose name has not been handed down but whose knowledge of the lie of the land and the habits of local people contributed realistically to the acquisition of fifty sites all within comfortable range of the brewery drays from Bridge Street, Reading.

Not everything went smoothly in the creation of these fifty new public houses, which was such a master stroke in the Simonds' fortunes. Loud protests came from a clergyman near Eversley. He declared that Mr. Simond's hunting days were doomed for the swamping of the countryside with beer-houses would surely destroy the trade of his brewery. Whether this protest was made on general moral grounds or because the parson considered his amenities threatened is not clear. But according to Barnard's account of the affair, Mr. Simonds indulged in a little game with his would be tormentor: "In those days skittles were permissible to the British rustic, and Mr. Simonds, who dearly loved a joke, saw his opportunity. He accordingly bought a field adjoining the rectory garden, where, a fortnight before the passing of the Act, he put up a shed and a four-cornered alley, during which operation the foundations of the intended beerhouse rapidly rose above the ground. One morning the parson came to Mr. Simonds, in anything but the mildest of tempers, to remonstrate with him on the subject. Mr. Simonds, who received the parson in his usual courtly style, and with great affability, replied, "Why, my friend, you have frequently told me that you objected to *public houses,* so I am erecting this beerhouse and skittle-alley for the benefit of your parishioners. I admit that it abuts on to your garden, but then you must remember that the rectory itself occupies the choicest position in the village, and I can hardly imagine that you wish to appropriate to yourself what you would deny to your poorer neighbours. The noise of 'twicers' or 'floorers' will, when you are once used to them, afford you genuine pleasure, all the more so that you have spared your parishioners a walk of over a mile to the 'Red Lion' for their enjoyment." Eventually Mr. Simonds settled the matter amicably with the clergyman, and they afterwards became the best of friends." There are several versions of this story but they all agree that it ended happily ever after; although it is difficult to see precisely how the clergyman's anger was assuaged.

As soon as his new enterprise was established, Blackall Simonds retired to the Isle of Wight, leaving his brothers to carry on the business. The geographical situation of the brewery had already begun to play an important part in associating Simonds beer with the British Army and promoting the cherished slogan "The Stuff for the Troops."

9

While the Simonds business was being consolidated at Reading in the first half of the nineteenth century, fundamental changes were taking place in the organisation and structure of the British Army. In the early part of the century the soldiers' food and drink was supplied by Sutlers who accompanied the army wherever it happened to be. This system had gradually been regularised into a pattern of regimental canteens. But at the time of the Crimean War in 1854 the Hon. Sir John Fortescue, a great authority on the subject, has written "... as of all previous wars ... for all comforts and luxuries the army depended upon private adventurers." He goes on to explain: "Vast changes, administrative and other, were effected in the Army during and immediately after the Crimean War, though the Indian Mutiny followed so closely upon it that the greater part of the Army was abroad, practically from 1854 till 1859. Foremost among these changes was the transfer of the Commissariat from the control of the Treasury to that of the War Office, and the establishment of what was called the Military Train, a forerunner of the present Army Service Corps."

This reorganisation of army catering arrangements meant that it was possible for a concern like Simonds to build up a military connection in the same way that brewers in Southwark and elsewhere had built up a trade with the navy. This of course was facilitated by the concentration of military forces in nearby Hampshire.

Aldershot was originally purchased as a military exercising ground in 1853. Queen Victoria and the Prince Consort rode over the site with Lord Hardinge who had acquired it for the Government, and it was said that the Prince pointed to part of the newly acquired land and said: it would be a pretty site for a camp." Hardinge treated this as a royal command and sited the camp there without further question. It was opened for militia in 1855. It was the first and for many years the only training area for military manoeuvres. "The idea of an exercising ground was excellent" writes Fortescue, "for in time of peace there was only one quarter in the British Isles – Dublin – where troops enough could be collected even for the drilling of a brigade. Furthermore the situation of Aldershot, strategically, was well chosen. But there seems to have been some halting between the two opinions whether Aldershot should be merely a training ground or a permanent station; and apparently the Crimean war decided that it should be more or less permanent. As a kind of compromise wooden huts were erected instead of stable build-ings, and thousands of pounds were wasted in throwing up these shelters of green timber, which were cramped, uncomfortable and, in the matter of married quarters, not too respectful of decency. In fact, as one member of Parliament truly described it, Aldershot became a kind of squatters village; and through extreme bad management, the undesirable population, which invariably haunts a camp, was able to settle down close to it and yet beyond the reach of control. For the camp was placed on the edge of the government's property; and the Government, having raised the value of the adjacent land, so to speak, against itself, was obliged later to buy it up at an excessive price. Altogether Aldershot at the outset was far from an attractive place.

Nevertheless the mere concentration of a comparatively large body of troops was productive of good to the soldier. At Aldershot crime diminished, while the general health of the men was bettered beyond precedent; and thus it was proved that with a little care the lives of thousands of men could be saved. Moreover, provisions could be bought in greater bulk and so retailed more cheaply to the rank and file. The soldiers were very suspicious of this latter change at first, but presently became reconciled to it, and then welcomed the improvement. The Commissariat, of which more shall be said later, was learning its business, and the bread which it issued at Aldershot was far superior to that baked in London. Gradually these benefits were extended to foreign stations . . ."

With Simonds owning property at Sandhurst an army connection had been made even before the Battle of Waterloo. In June 1814 Blackall Simonds had written a letter, which is still preserved, about the supply of beer to Sandhurst.

The letter is reproduced in the third illustrated section.

So, the records say, the victory at Waterloo was duly toasted at Sandhurst in Simonds' beer, and the firm was well placed for contracts for the supplies to the canteens of Aldershot, and to the public houses established there to serve the needs of the ever increasing static population.

During the second half of the nineteenth century Simonds became so closely associated with the army that they followed the troops overseas, establishing branches in Malta, Gibraltar, Egypt, South Africa and Cyprus.

The firm's connection with Malta, for instance, started with the appointment of an agent there, Mr. Hearn – a relative of the Simonds family – in 1875. The trade flourished and in 1890 a branch was established which ultimately became Simonds-Farsons, and from 1928 – when the brewery at Hamrun was built – was associated with a famous local enterprise and became known as Simonds-Farsons-Cisk. A similar development from an agency to a branch took place at Gibraltar where it ultimately became associated with Saccone & Speed Limited, renowned as suppliers to the armed forces, and now a part of the Courage Group.

In this country these developed a speciality in catering for the troops which became a byword. Not only the regular army but the militia and volunteer forces were much taken up with manoeuvres. Whenever the time and place of such excercises were rumoured it was always said "Simonds' man will know". The firm in fact developed an innocuous intelligence service in order to be on the spot with their barrels and bottles even before the military arrived to assuage the initial thirst, which was often the greatest thirst of all. To achieve this the brewery established a department for manufacturing tents and all the necessary field equipment, with teams expert in the erection of tents of all sizes to provide canvas canteens.

The summer manoeuvres of 1872 when Simonds supplied what were described as "the troops of flying columns" on Salisbury Plain made the firm's reputation in this speciality. In 1898 the Salisbury Plain operation was repeated on a much larger scale with the largest concentration of troops on West Down ever known. The consumption of beer was described as "colossal". Simonds not only used every horse in their extensive stable but had to hire every available horse in Reading. The first use of motor transport, however, came to their rescue when they undertook a contract for the manoeuvres in 1911 which extended from Aldershot and Salisbury Plain to the Eastern counties.

The connection with military needs was essentially flexible and withdrawals sometimes followed territorial gains. For instance, in 1889 an agent was appointed in the Sudan and a branch was opened there in 1908 and these subsequently disappeared. During the period of the Boer War there was a flourishing agency in Crete which has long since disappeared. While the British Army remained in Ireland there were branches in Dublin and Cork, both of which had to be closed down after being attacked during the rebellion.

A still active reminder of the Simonds association with Queen Victoria's Empire-building armies and their canvas canteens of the days before NAAFI is the still-flourishing tentage department at Reading. Here some old-timers together with the new generation of experts still manufacture and repair tents for erection for the sale of beer at outdoor sporting events, agricultural shows, etc. The mobility and flexibility developed by this firm, founded as it had been as a static localised rural industry, has been characteristic throughout its history. It was Simonds, for instance, which took on the formidable contract for supplying the British Empire Exhibition at Wembley in 1925. After the Second World War they reopened trade in Antwerp and acquired an interest in East African Breweries Ltd in Nairobi, Mombasa and Dar-es-Salaam.

10

The Reading firm, like the other elements in the Courage Group, maintained its strong family flavour. William Blackall Simonds lived within the precincts of the brewery during his active years. This was in the tradition of his time and it had been mentioned that his way of life lacked style. His residence was in fact designed and built by the great Sir John Soane, an intimate friend of his, and this was an early indication of the taste for the arts and intellectual pursuits which ran in the family. The spacious, well proportioned house, creeper-clad with its wide windows looking out on the brewery yard, had been transformed into offices by the time it was photographed, set among horse-drawn drays, in the eighteen-nineties. It was used by Barnard to illustrate his visit about 1890. While his account, written just before the Boer War, is, for the most part, sturdily factual, it shows how the business had prospered even before its great expansion which was to come in the twentieth century. He approached the story with a lyricism which must be quoted at least for its pleasingly nostalgic note: "It was early in the month of May when we left London, by the South Western Railway, to pay our promised visit to the Reading Brewery. The season of spring had arrived, at whose magic touch the drooping sensibilities of our nature are aroused, and the heart filled with sensations of waking pleasure. Although, physically, man knows not the renewing power of the seasons, yet his mind cannot fail to acknowledge their genial and invigorating influence.

How delighted we were to turn our backs upon the busy city and make for the country, there to inhale the restoring balms with which myriads of bursting germs and blossoms were loading the soft and vernal gale. As we proceeded on our journey, how we admired the verdure of the fields and trees, the expanded and beautiful foliage of the sinuous woodbine spreading through the hawthorn hedges, the mingled hues of green, and the insensible sweetness of early vegetation. We reached our destination long before we had fully enjoyed the sylvan beauty of the scenery through which we had so rapidly passed."

Having recovered from this ecstatic experience on the old Great Western Railway and admired the Soane architecture, Barnard got down to his usual meticulous survey of place and product: "Though their trade mark, the red 'Hop Leaf', is now so well known, we understand that Messrs. Simonds' first trial in brewing pale ale was eminently disastrous, from a financial point of view. Having made the experiment in a good strong bitter beer of the old-fashioned type, Messrs. Simonds duly consigned it to Melbourne, where it fetched quite a fabulous price. Unfortunately, the consignee stuck to the money, and had not the grace to return even the empty casks. Nothing daunted, however, the firm turned their attention to making this class of ale a speciality, and wisely cultivated a demand for it among their own more immediate connection.

At this period a taste for a lighter kind of ale had just set in; Messrs. Simonds therefore applied themselves to the task of producing a beer of much lower specific gravity, and on the identical principles now adopted at Burton and elsewhere, using a large quantity of the finest hops, and adopting what was then a novel expedient – hopping down with dry hops introduced into the casks.

To this beer they gave the name of S B, and so pronounced was its success, that the demand for it soon necessitated the reconstruction and enlargement of their brewery. Since that time the process of extension has gone on to the present day, until the brewery has become almost the largest provincial one in the South of England, and the premises cover seven acres of ground.

From any point of view the brewery buildings, on account of

their magnitude and picturesque appearance, are most striking, particularly the lofty new brewhouse on the river side of the premises. The plant of the old brewery has been remodelled to suit that of the new, which latter is of the most costly description, and either can be worked separately or both can be used together. It is only when one sees the inside of these vast establishments, with their ponderous engines and machinery, their great cellars filled with thousands of barrels of beer, that he can form any idea of the capital employed by the brewer in the production of a good glass of ale. During the last thirty years the Reading Brewery has assumed gigantic proportions, and the present proprietors can boast of having more than quadrupled its output since their advent to the business."

The men who were running the brewery with such success in the Victorian heyday were the grandsons of William Blackall Simonds, and their background is of some interest as it shows the unusual versatility in the talents they brought to the running of the business. The Chairman at that time was Henry John Simonds, a former Fellow of King's College, Cambridge, who had practised at the Bar. He became Mayor of Reading, a County Councillor and, characteristically, Secretary of the Local Hunt. But it was he who had been in charge of the prodigious operations of supplying the army manoeuvres.

With him on the Board was Henry Adolphus Simonds who had had commercial experience in America before joining the business in 1850. He also was Mayor of Reading and became Chairman of the County Brewers' Society.

The third Director, Blackall Simonds, began as a civil engineer working under Sir John Fowler on the construction of London's Metropolitan Railway. When he came into the family business he was responsible for great reconstruction works at Reading, his ideas being so original in their day that they attracted visits from London architects. He also became Mayor of Reading, High Sheriff of Berkshire and Chairman of the brewery between 1896 and 1905.

But the man who left his mark literally at Reading was

George Blackall Simonds who sculptured the great Lion which stands to this day in Forbury Gardens, as a memorial to the Berkshire men who fell in the Afghan War of 1880. He was also responsible for statues of Queen Victoria outside Reading Town Hall and his fellow industrialist George Palmer, the biscuit king, in Palmer Park. Born in 1843 he studied art in Dresden and Brussels and then went to live for twelve years in Rome. But like other members of the family he was drawn back to Reading and the family business. He was Chairman of the brewery from 1910 to the time of his death in 1929. He did not relinquish his interest in the arts which he combined with an enthusiasm for the revival of falconry.

Finally, the Secretary and Manager of the company at the time of Barnard's visit was Louis de Luze Simonds, one of whose sons became Lord Simonds, Lord Chancellor in 1951. His eldest son, popularly known as "Eric", entered the brewery as a trainee in 1902 and became Chairman in 1938. "He was the inspiration and driving force of the firm's growth from 300-350 public houses and one brewery in 1916 to 1,400 houses and four breweries in 1952." it was stated on the occasion of his brewing jubilee. Assets had risen from £778,000 in 1902 to nearly £10,500,000.

When he made his report Barnard met seven members of the Simonds family who were active in the business, and he concluded his account with this note of personnel: "There are employed, at Reading alone, six managers, three superintending brewers, a staff of twenty clerks, five travellers, and over 200 workmen. Adding to these the 170 persons employed at the firm's eleven branch houses in England, and those at Malta and Gibraltar, and the separate staff of 140 people engaged on their railway and pier contracts, it gives us a grand total of more than 500 persons, a number of which the proprietor of any business may well be proud."

At this period the company had already joined its future confederates on the Thames waterfront in London. Their depot was in a noble house in Grosvenor Road facing across the river to Lambeth Palace, having a wharf to which the beer was delivered direct from Reading, the upper reaches of the Thames still serving a useful commercial purpose. The business in London was already substantial for the nearby stables accommodated fifteen horses for metropolitan use.

Thus, toward the turn of the century, the firm – which like other breweries had been incorporated as a public company in the eighteen-eighties – had consolidated and spread far and wide. But a significant expansion was to come through mergers carried out later than those of most other companies of the Courage Group in the present century.

The first of these were the Tamar Brewery, Devonport, which was taken over in 1919, and the South Berks Brewery the following year. The big expansion throughout the south and west of England came in the thirties with the acquisition of Ashby's at Staines, Rogers of Bristol, Wheeler's Wycombe Breweries, Cirencester Brewery, Lakeman's Brewery, Brizham, Stiles of Brigend, and Marsh of Blandford. To these in the post-war years were added Bowley of Swindon, May of Basingstoke, Phillips of Newport (Mon.), Grant of Torquay, Blundell and The Octagon Brewery, Plymouth, and Pool of Penzance. Earlier in the century Simonds possessed a great array of branch offices, particularly associated with military and naval bases. But with the advent of motor transport, the need for these diminished and there was a general rationalisation of the pattern of the business.

The offices at Reading, rebuilt at the turn of the century, remained the pivot of the enterprise and are now the headquarters of Courage Central. Though there is still a Simonds presiding there, there are few relics of the past except in the memories of old hands. Soane's gracious building has disappeared, together with the stabling for the directors' carriages and horses, and the kennels for the Dalmatian carriage dogs which used to trot between the rear wheels. Until the beginning of the present reign barges still came to London bearing timber for casks; but as with other breweries the river frontage is no longer in commercial use, and gone too is the boathouse for the directors' river-craft.

When in 1960 Simonds joined the Courage Group they brought with them some 1200 tied houses, hotels and catering establishments as well as the chain of retail wine and spirit shops operating under the name of Arthur Cooper (Wine Merchant) Limited.

GEORGES

11

At the Western Headquarters of the Courage Group at Georges Brewery by Bristol Bridge there is preserved a worn leather-bound Cash Book. It is substantially thick but pocket-sized – that is to say it fitted well enough in the capacious eighteenth century flap-pocket of one who carried it constantly, used it assiduously for his business, domestic and even religious affairs, and thus leaves us a curious personal record of a man who went into brewing in Bristol a year after John Courage crossed the Thames at Southwark. Both of them turned to beer as a diversification in an already active life. A hundred and seventy three years later the two businesses built up by their descendants and successors were to merge.

The owner of the pocket Cash Book was Philip George who was thirty-eight years old and in a substantial way of business when he formed a partnership with six other notable Bristol merchants to establish a brewhouse by the bridge at Bristol in 1788, trading under the name of Philip George and the Bristol Porter Brewery.

Philip himself was a first generation Bristolian. His father having come from Worcester in 1736 to set up as a distiller in Baldwin Street. Philip, born in 1750 – the elder of two sons - - entered the family distillery and was thus connected from the beginning with the drink trade. Very soon he was involved also in dealings in hops and malt, but his most consistent venture, apart from financial flutters which appear in the extracts from his Cash Book, was the manufacture of lead shot.

He acquired this interest from William Watts, a Bristol plumber, who is said to have invented his patent lead shot as a result of a curious dream his wife had in the seventeen-sixties. Mrs. Watts awoke the good plumber – presumably in the morning – with a startling command: "go and fetch a ladle and some lead". Following a procedure conducted by her dream, she placed a bowl of water at the foot of the stairs, went to the top of the stairwell and emptied a ladle of molten lead through a colander. On striking the water the drops of lead became perfectly round. This remarkable experiment was celebrated in verse:

> Down from the staircase-head she throws small
>   drops of lead
> One fell on Watt's nose, 'twas scalding hot,
> The rest into the water cold
> In drops of perfect roundness roll'd
> And Watts with wonder did behold
> The birth of Patent Shot.

No doubt the story is apocryphal, but there is no doubting the fact that Watts took out a patent for his shot in 1782 and that a few years later an enterprise came into being called Watts, George and the Patent Shot Company.

By 1790 Philip George had taken over from the inventor and the concern became known as Philip George and the Patent Shot Company.

William Watts lived in Redcliffe Parade in Bristol, and his original shot tower has only recently been demolished. Happily full details including drawings and photographs of this item of industrial history have been preserved at Bristol Museum. Watt created it by taking part of the roof off his house, erecting a tower above it, and cutting holes through existing ceilings. He obtained the necessary length of drop for the larger size of shot by bringing into use a well, directly underneath the house, and which was as deep as the tower was high. Continuity has been maintained. The Sheldon Bush & Patent Shot Co. Ltd., to whom the business has descended, have erected a new shot tower just across the river from the brewery. Philip George's interest in the shot business was not, as it might appear, a side issue for this enterprise helped to carry him through the early years of his brewing – which frequently showed a loss.

Philip George dominated the affairs of the brewery during the period of its slow and difficult first decade of trading, and gradually established it firmly on its feet after the turn of the century. It is clear from the old Minutes that he was the active force in the partnership in spite of his many other interests. His partners, while taking some interest in the financial business such as Bills of Exchange, left the practical side of the brewing very much in his hands.

That Philip George had already had some practical experience before the brewery was founded is indicated in his mother's Will, dated 1782, in which he, as beneficiary, was described as "a maltster and brewer". This seems to imply that he had been in some way indirectly involved in one of the Bristol brewing enterprises while following his family business as a distiller. The 1788 foundation was not started from scratch. The partnership took over intact the Bristol Porter Brewery which had been built by Isaac Hobhouse and others about half a century before, at the end of the seventeen-thirties.

Isaac Hobhouse was one of the most famous of the Bristol slave traders. After his death his share of the brewhouse passed to his two nephews, John and Henry. John Hobhouse lived at Westbury-on-Trym and was the grandfather of the great Radical statesman, John Cam Hobhouse, Lord Broughton, who played a part in the passing of the Reform Bill in 1832. Though the Hobhouse family returned to brewing and indeed are still represented in the Courage Group, the Bristol brewhouse was sold to James Grimes in the latter part of the eighteenth century, and it was he who in turn sold to the Philip George partnership. It consisted then of the original brewhouse, a malthouse and a warehouse in Tucker Street. Originally there were eight equal shares in the concern at £2,000 each, but it appears, from a study of the Minutes of the first meeting on January 3rd 1788, that the number of shares was in fact seven, and that James

Morgan, who is named as the eighth partner in a draft Co-partnership Agreement, never actually took up his share.

The partners were mostly eminent Bristol merchants. Some were in the slave-trade, then a dominant feature of commercial life in the city. Indeed, two of the partners were involved in a public controversy on the "traffic" as it was called, on opposite sides. Mr. Peter Lunell was secretary of the first provincial committee set up to encourage legislation abolishing the slave-trade, and Mr. Samuel Span was a member of a committee of well-to-do local merchants defending "a traffic on which the welfare of the West India islands and the commerce and revenue of the Kingdom so essentially depend".

It is conjectural whether Messrs. Lunnell and Span ever became involved in arguments on this explosive subject in the Board Room. Certainly a great measure of Bristol's prosperity at that time was bound up in the slave-trade. One of its principal industries was the refining of sugar, many of the refineries being in and around Counterslip, Temple Backs and Tucker Street, and vessels often made a round trip from Bristol to Africa where the slaves were obtained, from thence to the West Indies where they were sold or bartered for raw sugar or rum, which was brought back to the city for refining or blending.

According to Latimer's Annals of Bristol, the year was not an auspicious one in which to enter the brewing trade. "With the year 1788", he wrote, "commenced a series of bad harvests and a long period of distress." Possibly because of this it was necessary for Philip George and the Bristol Porter Brewery to look beyond Bristol for the sale of their porter. On the 18th March, 1789, Mr. George told his partners that trade had been opened up with Ireland and with Liverpool, that 80 barrels of porter were being shipped to Cork, the same number to Waterford, and a further 100 barrels to Liverpool.

It was in the Bristol tradition of course to look west for trade, and Philip George seems to have realised from the start that the Irish market had great potential. Within five years of taking over the business he sent a traveller, John Bradley, on an Irish

23. Bristol's famous shot tower in Redcliffe Hill. The process was invented by William Watts of Bristol who saw it in a dream and then put it into practice. The tower of lath and plaster was erected over his own dwelling in the 18th century. He sold the process and the building to Philip George, founder of Georges Brewery and it has now been demolished to make way for an extensive road scheme.

24-28. This sequence shows some of the ways in which George's beers were transported during the first half of this century.

24. Two light engines "Oakhill" and "Mendip" transported Oakhill Stout across the Mendip Hills from the brewery to Binegar Station early this century. The locomotives were sold to a dock in South Wales, and are not, so far as is known in existence now.

25. A load of Oakhill Stout on its way from the brewery in the Mendips to Binegar railway station at the turn of the century. From 1904 onwards the steamers were superseded by two small locomotives, "Mendip" and "Oakhill".

26. The Georges fleet of ten
steam wagons in the
brewery yard at Bristol. The
Period is the 1920's.

27. The last of the Georges'
Greys.

28. Motorised transport in
the 1920's at the Bristol
Brewery Georges.

26

27

GEORGES BEERS.
GEORGES BEERS.
beer is best
beer is best

Georges

29. A group at the Oakhill
Brewery in 1880. George's
acquired this Brewery in
1925.

30. Edward Bird's drawings
of George's Brewery in
1932.

31. Reproduction of an advertisement for Best Old Porter from Philip George and the Bristol Porter Brewery in 1816.

BEST. OLD. PORTER.

AT

FOUR PENCE HALFPENNY

Pr QUART.

15. July 1816.

Reproduced from old copper plate now in the possession of The Company

tour to promote the company's porter. The journey lasted for five fatiguing months. Bradley wrote a journal, the text of which unfortunately has been lost, though some extracts survive. Arthur Hadley, former Managing Director and Head Brewer of Georges, who had read it stated that: "It constitutes not only an interesting contemporary record of the competition of Bristol, London and Liverpool firms in supplying Ireland with beer and of the early days of the Irish brewing industry, but is a document of historical value, as it throws many sidelights on Irish life of that period." Bradley had left Bristol in January 1792. "By the middle of February, Bradley reached Waterford, where he had some successful interviews with large firms, but saw that a Liverpool Company would prove a dangerous competitor. Horseback was then the only method of getting over the ground, and 20 miles a day was as much as a traveller could do. He visited various small towns, and on one occasion completely lost his way. Eventually we find him at Cork on 26th February, where he was received 'with great politeness.' Among the many that he interviews was one Edward Haynes of whom he writes:

"'I find he began with but little, but is believed to be worth money and still getting forward rather rapidly, and no wonder, for besides being an active pushing man in business, he calls in the powerful aid of various Spirits, and being well acquainted with them, I'm informed they assist him greatly, and on his part, if they at times happen to be weak, it seems with great readiness he'll strengthen them, in return for services rendered him, thus mutually supporting each other.'

"Haynes was persuaded to take 500 barrels and Bradley, after other successful negotiations, wrote:

"'It is likely you will have, at least for the present, a good sale here for, I'm informed Cork imports 60,000 barrels annually.'

"He reached Limerick on March the 6th, 1792, where he found the people 'rather against the Bristol Porter.' At Galway on March the 11th, he records that: 'people here complain of the colour being too deep, but approve of the body, which they

105

acknowledge considerably superior to the London, therefore they mix them to make the London better and sell it as London Porter where they can, tho' some will prefer at the Pot Houses the Bristol Porter and ask for it as such, which is a proof of its gaining ground here.'

"His accounts of Irish inns and cabins, where he often slept on the floor or sat all night by a turf fire, of the pride, sensitiveness and poverty of his hosts, of the appalling state of the roads, and many other impressions, form a remarkable pen picture of Ireland at that time."

12

Meanwhile an important figure in the affairs at Bristol was Arthur Tozer who, at one of the earliest Board Meetings held at the Assembly Coffee House in November 1788, was appointed Manager and Conductor of the business with responsibility for keeping Books of Account. His salary was £150 a year, augmented by an "allowance of House Rent, Coal, Candle and Beer." Tozer was active in getting the business on to its feet. But by 1800 when it was doing well – though his salary had been increased – he was disappointed in not being able to obtain a stake in the business, and it was noted in the Minutes that he had resigned his position, his "efforts to obtain a Share having been unsuccessful."

In 1790 the partners received an offer from one of their members to purchase the brewhouse and after two years in business it is significant that they did not close the door to this possibility, stating that they were unwilling to dispose of it "at least for the present." It was in that year that they decided that the brewing of porter was not enough and they started a Pale Ale Brewery taking over "Bayly's Premises" for "fitting up and applying . . . for the purpose of carrying on the brewing business." This expansion was done at some risk as the concern showed a loss of £150 for the year 1790/1791.

Before the turn of the century they did not make their own malt, but in 1795 Mr. Tozer was sent to Berkshire and Hertfordshire to make enquiries regarding the method of making brown malt and to observe the construction of malt kilns. A model was produced and it was resolved that enquiries be made for a malt house to rent. Four years later they were still importing malt for the Minutes refer to a mishap, not uncommon in those days: "Mr. Tozer acquainted the Committee that the Brig Daniel on which we have 340 Quarters of Malt shipped by Mr. Warren, was, on the night of the 27th grounded on the rocks called The Wolves in Bristol Channel and afterwards run into Uphill River where she now lies with hopes however of getting into this port."

This maritime touch was characteristic of Philip George's business in the early days. The brewery was well sited by the bridge and transport by water, significant in most breweries until the present century, played a vital part in the economy of the Bristol concern.

In Philip George's day the roads in the west country were in such an appalling state that any widespread distribution of beer was out of the question. By all accounts the streets of Bristol itself were worse even than those of London in their narrowness, filth and congestion. Much of the city's traffic was carried by water, and Bristol Bridge was in a very real sense the hub of the city. The proximity of George's with the bridge and the harbour was of inestimable value both at the time and throughout the nineteenth century. Though the river frontage has fallen into disuse, like the Thames frontages at Horselydown, London, the brewery still flourishes as the west of England headquarters of the Courage Group on the site of the original Porter Brewery.

The minutes of the old Porter Brewery kept by Philip George and his partners recalled much detail of the daily life of the business but curiously contain no reference to an event on the bridge in 1793 in which they must have been involved, at least as witnesses. This was the Bristol Bridge Riots, the most tragic local incident of the century. According to Latimer the cause of the upheaval was the failure of the Trustees of the Bridge to abolish the toll-houses (and with them, of course, the tolls) at either end of the bridge. Eleven persons were killed or mortally wounded and 45 others injured, and, as is always the case with such calamities several of the sufferers were harmless lookers-on, two being respectable tradesmen and one a visitor to the city. Perhaps the Minutes which were so meticulously kept omitted all mention of this because no damage was done to the brewhouse and the employees came through unscathed. But they did reflect the fact that the company was much taken up with banking matters which so often co-existed with brewing. There are many references to the issue, backing and endorsing of Bills of Exchange. A typical Minute is one dated 5th April 1803 when "Mr. Spiring reported he had taken up Two Thousand five hundred pounds on the Company's note at 3 mo., of Messrs. Miles Vaughan & Co., and had therewith paid the Company's note to Mr. Jas. Fowler for the same sum, the 27th Mar."

Something of the diversity of interest which sometimes went with brewing at the turn of the eighteenth century is to be found in that pocket book which Philip George carried for most of his active life. For instance there were his dealings with two of his Porter brewery partners, W. P. Lunell and Samuel Worrall of Clifton. About 1800 he paid Samuel Worrall out as a partner with his share in "Wilder Street premises", £150 cash from profits on Shot Ho. and 2 shares in "the Coal Canal." His share in Neh. Bartley & Co., a distillery on Temple Backs, he transferred to W. P. Lunell in 1791, but only received from him about half its value, which may have terminated their business relationship.

As an adjunct to his Patent Shot Company he acquired a lead Works in Blackwirth Road, Bristol, and shares in lead mines near Helston – the "Wheal Prosper" and the "Wheal Rose". He also traded in liquor other than beer. He bought large quantities of rum, brandy and port and the excise was considerable. For instance:

"Wm. Morgan: Duty on Rum £457. 6. 0d.
M. R. Hunter on a/c of Rum £1,446. 9. 10d."

He had a moiety of a Yard in Jacob Street, bought 2 small horses for £31. 10. 0d. and 3 coach horses for £68. 5. 0d., exported patent shot to Hy. Cruger, New York; porter, lead and shot to Gibraltar (they paid him in "dollars"), and indulged in an "adventure to Maryland" which produced £458. 15. 6d. A promissory note in the name of H. O. Wills for £209. 6. 6d. *may* be on account of tobacco.

From 1787 to 1791, he was in partnership with T. Corser and William Fisher in a wine business which involved chiefly brandy, raisins and excise. In various places appear the words "colouring", "wages", "halling", "masons", "£16. 16. 0d. for a Prefs." and "coopering". He had shares in the "Newbury canal" and Bills of Exchange played a great part in his dealings. He obviously visited London, Wales, Cornwall, Plymouth.

He bought a horse, bridle and saddle from one William Turner for £40, paid his Moiety in a Cloth Cottage at Devizes (£7. 3. 6d.), purchased premises in various streets, bought a "pillion and portmanteau" for £1. 13. 0d. and was closely connected with St. Stephen's parish. He paid the ringers 15/-d periodically, the Sexton for mops and brushes and cleaning up the church and there is a payment (unspecified) to the late Churchwarden of £265. 14. 4d. Plumbers are also paid and the Sexton is paid for "lighting ye Stove".

One of the more curious names is that of Jonadab Mort of Liverpool. He seems to have been closely associated with the firm of Lewis Corser and Harford, Bristol. In 1796 George paid John Champion of Bristol £200 as "my moiety $\frac{1}{2}$ years. Rent on the Mill."

Certainly the diversifications of Philip George and his partners were necessary for the brewery showed a profit for the first time only in 1797, nearly ten years after they took over. But from then on a profit was sustained, shared at first by four partners, then three, and at last two, as they either died or retired from the business. From time to time there were disagreements. In 1798 there was a row about the distribution of profit. Apparently Philip George had not fully paid up his share of the capital. Mr. Sam Worrall was agitator and there is a note in the Minutes "N.B. Mr. Philip George being present refused to sign the above."

Two years later the Minute Book itself was a cause of

disagreement. Mr. Worrall had put pressure on Philip George to pay up his capital and had succeeded and now he was worried about the location and safety of the Minute Book. The co-partners did not take him very seriously and the book continued to be kept in the usual place, wherever that was.

The trading figures for the forty years of Philip George's management - he died in 1828 – reflect a very slow but steady growth. The export trade seemed always to have been a variable factor. In some months it was as high as 257 barrels (795 in February 1795), in other months nothing at all. Possibly it depended on whether there was a local market or not. Certainly it is noticeable that in Winter, when local trade was lowest, export tended to rise. In August, 1800, trade reached a peak of 2,462 barrels (inclusive of town, country and export) but thereafter declined slightly. By 1828, the average monthly barrelage was in the region of 1,000. Though there were, of course, considerable seasonal fluctuations, with February invariably the lowest at about half the barrelage of the summer months. A special export beer was brewed in 1795; some of the barm being sent to Richard Clare of Cork who had a distillery there. In 1802 the firm was bottling cider and perry as well as porter and ale. But porter was still predominant. When peace was declared in that year, Philip George produced one of his slogans which was widely advertised:-

"PEACE, PLENTY AND PORTER"

A Wages Book covering the period from 1821 to 1828 provides some sidelights on management. Written in a handsome copperplate, it gives details of wages paid to coopers, warehouse and cellar men. Much of the payment was piece work especially that involving the washing of casks, vessels and bottles. The basic weekly rate ranged from 13/-d to 19/6d, the highest rate being paid to the coopers. The total weekly wage bill was in the region of £22.

There were fines for improper language to the Brewers (1/-d), getting drunk (2/6d) and for being late on brewing morning

(1/-d). On December 21st 1822, a character called William Haynes was fined Sunday's wages for leaving the large plug out. He appears to have been an unsatisfactory employee, since in March 1823 he had to be discharged for "seducing William Howe's daughter". William Howe was another employee.

Before the end of 1816 all the original partners had disappeared with the exception of Philip George and Jacob Wilcox Ricketts, who decided to retire in favour of their sons. A new partnership was then formed being styled Georges, Rickettses and Co. A drawing of the period shows the porter and the pale ale breweries as separate buildings. The quayside, with horse-drays, barges and sailing trows underlines the continued importance of the river frontage in Bristol.

The new partnership announced itself in a circular dated October 1st 1816: "Messrs. Philip George, Jun., Richard Ricketts, Christopher George, Jacob Ricketts, Henry Ricketts, Alfred George and Frederick Ricketts, respectfully announce that they have taken to the business of Porter-Brewers, lately carried on by Messrs. Philip George, Sen. and Jacob Wilcox Ricketts, and that such business will in future be carried on by them at the Brewery and premises in Bath Street, Bristol, under the firm of 'Georges, Ricketts', and Bristol Porter Brewery Company'.

"Referring you to the above advertisement, we respectfully solicit a continuance of the support enjoyed by our predecessors, and assure you that no exertion shall be wanting for the prompt and careful execution of your orders.

"We are further determined to merit a preference by vending on liberal terms, Porter, Strong Beer, and West India Ale, of quality superior to most Breweries, and inferior to none in the Kingdom.

      "We are,

     "Your obliged and most obedient Servants,   "

This was the period when the Company began to acquire its own licensed houses and so, to some extent at least, free itself from the fierce and unremitting competition between brewers that drove many small breweries into liquidation. A typical case, locally, was that of Fry, Ball & Co. Their old letter-book covering the last years of the concern is still extant. It contains the statement that "Our Porter is generally allow'd to be superior to the London brew'd, and we doubt not will have a great sale in your neighbourhood if one tried. Our strong beer is in equal repute." Of course, this is sales talk, and though the Frys were Quakers it is evident from the letters that they were also men of business who could drive a hard bargain. There is a liberal sprinkling of Thee's, Thou's, wast and can'st, but in the collection of their accounts, Fry, Ball & Co. do not appear to be behindhand. One of their descendants, incidentally, was Conrad Fry, who was on the board of Georges, and is still remembered by some of the staff.

Family continuity has been as strong at Bristol as at Southwark and Reading. Members of the George family were active in the business until the retirement of Mr. Christopher George in 1951. Philip George – the founder – like his contemporaries in Southwark and Reading, played his part in public life being a Sheriff of Bristol in the years 1808, 1813 and 1815.

13

The second generation of Georges and Rickettses seemed to have dominated the partnership until the time of Philip George's death. Then they were joined by Richard Vaughan who belonged to a well known Bristol family of merchants and bankers. The Vaughans, in the course of time, replaced the Ricketts. When the last of that family died in 1860, £10,000 was paid out to his executors as a share of the capital. When the firm was incorporated as a limited company exactly one hundred years after its foundation, in 1888, Philip Henry Vaughan became the first Chairman of the Bristol Brewery Georges & Co., Ltd., as it was styled. A century of trading had built up a solid and substantial organisation. No wonder the public subscribed £6,300,000 in the first five hours of the first day of the public offer. The prospectus had stated that "The objects of the Company are to acquire, work and extend the well-known business of Georges & Co., Old Porter Brewery, Bristol, which is one of the largest Brewery businesses in the West of England, having been established just 100 years since by the ancestors of the present partners.

"The retirement of the Senior Partner at an advanced age, and the death of one of the Managing partners, make its present proprietors the more inclined to offer their business as a public investment and security.

"While it is manifest that the profits of a business of this class must vary in the future as well as in the past, the average profit of the last ten years gives the following result:-

"Average Profit last ten years £43,778

"The business is conducted at Bath Street, Bristol, The

Brewery premises are large and commodious with waterside frontage, enabling Malt and Coal barges to discharge direct into the Brewery ...

"The business consists of brewing Vatted beers (for which this Brewery has long been celebrated), Mild Beers, Bitter Ales and Stouts.

"In addition to its general trade, the Company will acquire 70 licensed houses, of which 63 are Freehold, and 7 Long Lease-hold, all free from Mortgage. There are also a number of Public and Beer Houses under obligation by loans and mortgage advances, besides about a dozen licensed houses leased to the Brewery."

The success of Georges in going public made a deep impression upon other brewery concerns in the locality. Indeed, it inspired three local brewery firms and one local brewery company to form the Bristol United Breweries Limited, which was incorporated a year later in 1889 and which was to become a chief rival of Georges for more than sixty years.

The story of both concerns until their merger in 1956 follows parallel lines of expansion, both by the build-up of trade and by the takeovers which have been so characteristic of the brewery industry since the eighteenth century.

In the year following their incorporation Georges took over the Bedminster Brewery. Many smaller breweries were afterwards absorbed – The Bath Brewery Co., Ltd.; Walton Brewery Co., Ltd.; Hall & Sons, the Lodway Brewery; John Arnold & Sons, Wickwar; and the Ashton Gate Brewery Co., Ltd. Until 1910 United and Georges were running neck and neck; then Georges took over the houses of R. & W. Miller and steadily drew ahead. During this half-a-century of steady growth Georges retained its very personal character, and the atmosphere of the concern is well reflected in the recollections of F. E. Long who joined the firm in 1910 at 12/-d a week and ultimately became Senior Brewer. "A few incandescent gas lamps, but mostly naked gas-burners and tallow dips ... In the Brewing Room, however, it was quite bright and warm, and I was greeted by Mr. Philip George, who was Mashing that day. He gave me a pile of loading lists, and told me to balance them with the Stores Stock Books, which at that time were kept by the Brewery Foreman. As I did not know how many firkins went to a barrel it was rather difficult, but I soon learnt. I have always found that the best way to learn a job is with the minimum instruction, think it out for yourself. In addition, I had work in the brewery, checking temperatures, et., general office-boy work, laboratory work, and assistance with the wages. Doing this job, I realised that the Directors were concerned with welfare in those early days. The wages (minimum) were 18/-d per week, 6. a.m. to 6. p.m.; 6. a.m. to 2. p.m. on Saturdays. The wages, though apparently small, were 2/-d a week higher than comparable employment in other firms. There was another matter which I thought extremely good for those days. Once a man was recognised as a permanent employee, he was granted during sickness two days pay per week. This compares very favourably with present-day Sickness Benefit, and was a gift and not paid for as at present. There was also a bonus of 1d in the £ for each 1% of dividend."

Mr. Long includes in his reminiscences an interesting note on the relationships between the rival brewery concerns. "In the early days there were conditions of strict secrecy, on account of so-called 'trade secrets'. I could not understand this, as there were many text-books by brewers and consultants long before this – I have one dated 1885.

"This secrecy was so strictly enforced that once, when I had to take a message to Mr. Cann ('Bristol Bill') at the United Brewery, I was told to go in at the back entrance and straight to the Brewer's Office. I felt like a thief in the night. This attitude did not change until the early part of the Great War, when brewers had to give all kinds of information in order to make the best use of materials, then in short supply."

This traditional air of secrecy was certainly manifest again in 1956 when negotiations between the two great rival breweries began. The idea of a merger was not entirely novel since

Georges had approached Bristol United at the beginning of the century and again in the nineteen-twenties. When Mr. A. C. Hadley, Chairman of Georges, began his talks with Mr. A. R. Boucher, a director of Bristol United and son of its Chairman, negotiations were conducted in private houses. "The secret was very well kept; the parties indeed did not even entrust clerical work to confidential clerks in the normal way, and the drafting of the transfer terms was effected and copied in manuscript by the members of one Board or the other. No whisper of the impending amalgamation had been given until the formal announcement was made in February 1956. Yet it was typical of the brewery industry in the west country that the amalgamation had all the characteristics of a friendly treaty. Indeed, it brought back to Georges Brewery one of the family names that had been associated with it from the very beginning. It was Isaac Hobhouse who had at first built a brewery on that site in 1730. His descendant Mr. H. C. Hobhouse came over from Bristol United to become a director of Georges.

When Bristol United started as a public company in 1889 they had not fared so well as Georges, at least not through press support. One London newspaper whose request for the advertisement of the prospectus had been turned down, published a lengthy attack on the issue headed "A Queer Beer Prospectus". Public support nevertheless was forthcoming, and B.U.B. Limited were soon launched on a career of expansion and acquisition which began with their takeover in 1897 of Daniel Sykes & Company Limited, proprietors of the Redcliff Brewery, one of Bristol's oldest having been established in 1753.

Many of the records of B.U.B. were destroyed in the German air attacks on Bristol in 1940. One curious detail preserved from the beginning of this century concerns the original auditors who had looked after the company since its inception. At the Annual General Meeting in 1902 this firm made the unexpected announcement that it did not seek re-election. It seems that the partner responsible for the brewery accounts had aligned himself with various teetotal interests in presenting a memorial

117

to the local Justices containing severe strictures upon the Licensed trade, and his conscience forbade him to continue to benefit professionally from beer. Strict teetotalism, however, began to flag as the century wore on, and at the time of the amalgamation the auditors were restored to look after the affairs of Georges.

Two amalgamations of special significance to B.U.B. took place during the present century, the acquisition in 1925 of the Oakhill Brewery and of the Charlton Brewery in 1937.

The village of Oakhill in the Mendips was a remote, almost unlikely setting for an important enterprise. Yet it was already flourishing in the eighteenth century, having been founded in 1767. The Rev. John Collinson in his history of Somerset published in 1791, referring to the parish of Ashwick, wrote: "A great part of the hamlet of Oakhill lies within this parish . . . it is now only famous for a large Brewery carried on with a great reputation by Messrs. Jordan and Billingsley and both these gentlemen have good houses there."

It is known that Jordan left the business and that Billingsley carried on until his death in 1811 when he was succeeded by W. P. Jillard. Oakhill Cottage which was Jillard's home was demolished in 1872 as not being grand enough for its then owner; while Billingsley's house, Ashwick Grove, was demolished in 1956 as being too large and grand for everyday use. The Jillards dropped out and the Spencer family came in and were in command when the concern went public like so many others in 1889. To celebrate the inauguration of the Oakhill Brewery Co., Ltd., a grand dinner was held inside a 500 barrel vat.

The following year maltings were established at Oakhill covering not only the needs of the brewery but supplying other breweries at Shepton Mallet and Bristol. But the product which became so famous that it was sold all over the country was Oakhill Invalid Stout. A pair of traction engines maintained a line of communication between the brewery and the nearest rail-head at Binegar. They were sometimes hard-pressed for in its heyday the output of the Oakhill Brewery was between 2,000 and 2,500 barrels a week. Because they damaged the roads of Mendip, they were replaced, in 1904, by a 3' gauge railway-line between Oakhill and Binegar, on which two engines called "Oakhill" and "Mendip" pulled truckloads of Oakhill stout. This intriguing little line was dismantled in 1919, when engines, rolling stock and track were sold to the contractors who were at that time constructing Barry Docks.

The descendants of Isaac Hobhouse became connected with the Oakhill Brewery at the beginning of the present century. Mr. H. C. Hobhouse writes: "My father, Mr. (later Sir) Reginald A. Hobhouse had married the daughter of Mr. F. Spencer, but the Hobhouse family had in fact been connected with brewing for a considerable time, my great-great-grandfather having been a Managing Partner in Whitbread's Brewery in 1800. The Hobhouse family were related by marriage to the Jillard family, for when, in 1872, my grandfather first met Mr. F. Spencer, he had come to Oakhill to settle up the affairs of a Mrs. Jillard, for whom he was an executor. It was this meeting that eventually led him to ask Mr. F. Spencer to take his son, my father, into the business in 1904".

The First World War, with its restrictions on the use of grain and difficulties in distribution from such a relatively remote base, led to a decline in this remarkable village industry. A disastrous fire in 1925 – how often these fires change the course of brewing history – dealt a fatal blow to Oakhill and the business was taken over by Bristol United. But the industry at Oakhill has not waned. The maltings were maintained by their new owners and are now with modern equipment, an important element in the activities of the Courage Group.

The Charlton Brewery at Shepton Mallet was another venture which flourished from deep country roots. During the eighteenth century when the wool trade was still thriving in Shepton Mallet, the factory was built at Charlton on the outskirts close to a spring which supplied pond water sufficient to drive the water-wheels. By the beginning of the nineteenth century the wool

119

trade had declined and the factory fell into disuse. But it was solid and well sited and the active spring of good water attracted the attention of Francis Berryman, the son of a wine and spirit merchant in Wells who had carried on a small brewery concern in that town in conjunction with the family business. He decided to open a new brewery at Charlton and took as his partner William Bide who was in the glove business in Yeovil – then the centre of glove-making. The firm was designated Bide and Berryman, but its management was entirely in the hands of Francis Berryman, who took over with the factory a dwelling house, yard, stabling, eight cottages, a 'plantation', two large ponds and the water-powered equipment which that served. When he arrived in 1844 he built No. 1 Malthouse by the millpond and No. 1 Cellar by the yard. The wages account for this work shows that the 'walling masons' were paid 8/-d a week and the 'banker' masons and carpenters 18/-d a week.

For the first decade it was a struggle to make the business pay. But between 1856 and 1886 things greatly improved. The Bide family withdrew in 1865 and Charles R. Burnell, an enterprising young man with good brewing experience, became a partner in the following year.

Between 1866 and 1884 the business expanded considerably and the name changed again to Berryman, Burnell & Co. When it became a limited company in 1886, C. R. Burnell was Chairman with two Berrymans as Directors. The two families continued in active management until the merger with the B.U.B. in 1937. At the time of writing the Charlton property is still in use as a depot for the Courage Group. It is inevitable that the placid self-sufficient life of such enterprises should taper with the increased pressures and need for centralisation in this century. The mill pond is still pretty but covered with vegetation. The water-wheels have long since ceased to play their part in the production. Though the factory premises and the yards are still full of activity the elegant brewer's house stands empty in its walled garden. After being a private residence it served its time as brewery offices but now, in its empty well-proportioned rooms, an atmosphere of spacious good living still lingers. One can well imagine some former occupant as a rustic Thrale who enjoyed elegance and good comfort but who nevertheless kept open his pass door to the brewery yard so that he could slip away at all times to keep an eye on the brewing and make his important decisions.

Bristol United Breweries and its Oakhill and Charlton sub-sidiaries and other acquisitions by Georges notably Hall & Sons of Lodway (acquired in 1911) and the Ashton Gate Brewery (acquired in 1932) provide other examples of family continuity. Reference has already been made to Captain Isaac Hobhouse and to the Hobhouse family. Mr. H. C. Hobhouse was a director of B.U.B. at the time of its acquisition by Georges and became a director of Georges. Mr. Charles Robert Hancock. a director of the Redcliff Brewery. Daniel Sykes & Company Limited, one of the early constituents of the B.U.B. became a director of B.U.B. and was joined there by his son-in-law, Mr. G. H. Boucher who later became its Chairman. He, in his turn, was joined by his son, Mr. A. R. Boucher who ultimately became a director of Georges. The three generations of this family were all Solicitors. On the acquisition of the Lodway concern Mr. Joseph Hall became a director of Georges. His brother Frank joined the staff later becoming a member of the board and, after the First World War, Joint Managing Director. On his death in 1926 he was succeeded by Mr. Joseph Hall, father of Mr. John Hall a director of Courage (Western) Ltd. Similarly, Mr. Inman Harvey and Mr. William Harvey became directors of Georges following the acquisition of their family business, the Ashton Gate Brewery Co., Ltd., in 1932.

Such units as Oakhill and Charlton had gone to build up the strength of B.U.B. and there was a Hobhouse and a Burnell on the Board when the amalgamation with Georges took place in 1956.

The merger of the two giants of West Country brewing did away with much redundancy and duplication. It was a well consolidated integrated organisation which joined the Courage Group, a year after the arrival of Simonds, in 1961.

JOHN SMITH'S of TADCASTER

14

The arrival of the nineteen-seventies added a significant northern dimension to the Group and some rich new facets of character. The interests of John Smith's Tadcaster Brewery which merged with those of Courage in October, 1970, included some 1800 pubs, hotels and freehold clubs – spread over Yorkshire, Lancashire, Derbyshire, County Durham, Cheshire, Lincolnshire, Nottinghamshire and parts of Cambridgeshire and Shropshire.

The origins of the John Smith's Group were diverse, stemming from the eighteenth century like other members of the Courage Group but contrasting in character and in the nature of its historical build-up over the years. Whereas the concerns in London, Reading and Bristol were closely related to rivers as a means of transportation and to a metropolitan and agricultural population growth, the Tadcaster enterprises were related to a road and were much concerned with industrial growth.

There is an historical link between Southwark and Tadcaster which is very direct. Though it is not immediately relevant to brewing history it is of significance to the foundation of both places. It is the Roman road system which crossed the Thames at Southwark close to the Anchor Brewery and which passes the gates of the Tadcaster Brewery on its way to York.

The existence of this ancient highway and of abundant springs of water at Tadcaster led to the establishment of breweries in that town in mediaeval times. When the township was the Roman staging post it was called Calcaria, a direct reference to the magnesium limestone rocks at Tadcaster which yield a hard water rich in sulphate of lime, comparable to the natural water of Burton which became renowned for brewing.

There is no evidence to show that the Romans themselves made beer at Tadcaster though the records of the 9th and the 6th Legions, both based in York, are well documented. It is known, however, that there were two breweries or brew-houses at Tadcaster in 1341 – one of them paid 8*d* in taxes that year and the other 4*d*. In about 1400 the best ale sold for 1½*d* per gallon but a century later the price had risen to 3*d* a gallon.

Another similarity in the placing of Southwark and Tadcaster in the Roman and mediaeval setting is that they were both on the approaches to bridges of strategic and commercial importance. Though the Tadcaster Brewery lies on the highway well away from the bridge and has very rarely resorted to water transport, the town owes much of its importance, as did old Southwark, to the crossing of the river – the Wharfe – first by a Roman ford, later by a bridge which was of strategic significance for instance at the time of the Civil War when the Battle of Marston Moor was fought nearby.

The old Roman road has of course continued as a great turnpike highway and it was natural that successions of inns and resting houses should have been built along its route. Five inn-keepers are recorded as being in business in Tadcaster in 1378. The place was also a post town with a post office registered in the time of Charles I for regular communication between London and York. There is plenty of evidence too that the carriage of mail, treasure and wealthy personages led to the highway being a target for robbery with violence. When the sum of 2050 marks was conveyed from London to York in 1319, a journey taking ten days, the guard from London to Huntingdon was eight horsemen, but on reaching the neighbourhood of Tadcaster this was increased to eleven horsemen and twelve able archers on foot, all armed and equipped with tipped arrows. It was Robin Hood country.

By the eighteenth century Tadcaster was enjoying great prosperity as a post town. In the hey-day of coaching some fifty stage coaches passed through and more than thirty of them changed horses in the town daily. These were augmented by great numbers of post-chaises and private vehicles of all kinds.

Very active in the coaching business were Messrs Backhouse and Hartley, partners in the small brewery which eventually came into the hands of John Smith. Together they horsed the York and Liverpool mail coach and the York and Liverpool "Highflyer". On alternate days they horsed the "Alexander", another Liverpool coach providing a team for the fifteen mile journey from Tadcaster to Leeds, the same team bringing back the return coach the same night. In 1777 Backhouse took over Tadcaster's leading coaching inn, the White Horse, where four of the eight London stage coaches, four in each direction, were horsed daily. On his own account Hartley was originally postmaster at Tadcaster in the days before the mails were carried by coach. In 1786 when the change took place he and his son set up a posting establishment to horse the Royal Mails between Tadcaster and York. He seems to have been a diversifier for he also had a share in Deacon Harrison & Co., who operated heavy baggage-wagons – "slow-coaches" – and he is recorded as horsing the well-known Leeds and Scarborough coach, the "Prince Blucher".

But the one asset of lasting value which these shrewd men of business created was their brewery. The Industrial Revolution swept across the north of England and brought in its wake the railroads which dramatically swept away the valuable coaching traffic from the old Roman road. The coaching inns of Tadcaster had been closing their doors for some years when the railway reached the town in 1847 and Tadcaster had begun to have the appearance of a ghost town. The brewery however remained. The partners did not live to see the building of the railway station and by that time the business had passed into the hands of Jane Hartley and it was from her representatives that John Smith acquired it in 1847.

Smith was only 24 years old when he took on the somewhat daunting task of nursing a run-down brewery in a depressed town to meet the demands of a changing world. The measure of his success was that, at the time of his death in 1879, he and his partners were planning the building of a new brewery at a cost of £130,000 which opened and flourished a few years after his death.

It is difficult to specify any one reason for John Smith's success. Like so many young men who made good in the earlier part of the nineteenth century – and contrary to general belief it was a young man's world – he seems to have been imbued with remarkable energy, much versatility, and a gift for recognising the needs of changing times. He diversified, farming extensively, feeding fat cattle on a fairly large scale, and involving himself with the limestone quarries for which Tadcaster was famous (having supplied much stone for York Minster). As a brewer he was keenly aware of, but undaunted by, the booming breweries of Burton-on-Trent. He saw in their success opportunities for the modernisation and expansion of the hitherto localised Tadcaster business. With his brother William who was to succeed him, he set out to furnish a product of the quality that changing public taste demanded, a clear beer which was becoming popular with the replacement of the traditional pint mug by the glass.

Not least of his qualities was an ability to choose the right man and to create good working conditions as the concern grew and spread. He employed Joseph Grimston, a rule-of-thumb brewer of the old school who was, nevertheless, a gold-medal-winner. Grimston was an individualist who insisted on doing things with his own hands, grinding the malt, mashing, running the wort into the copper, seeing it boiled and himself pumping it from the copper to the coolers. He was succeeded as Head Brewer by Percy Clinch who was appointed by H. H. Riley-Smith and who belonged to a later school of scientific brewing. It was Clinch who managed to overcome the suspicion that lingered in the minds of consumers that there could be anything wrong with a beer that was bright and clear. It was in Clinch's time, too, that John Smith's was among the first to establish its own laboratory, its equipment being described in early records as "paraphernalia". It is often said at Tadcaster

YORK Four Days Stage-Coach.

Begins on Friday the 12th of April 1706.

ALL that are desirous to pass from *London* to *York*, or from *York* to *London*, or any other Place on that Road; Let them Repair to the *Black Swan* in *Holbourn* in *London*, and to the *Black Swan* in *Coney-street* in *York*.

At both which Places, they may be received in a Stage Coach every *Monday*, *Wednesday* and *Friday*, which performs the whole Journey in Four Days, (*if God permits.*) And sets forth at Five in the Morning.

And returns from *York* to *Stamford* in two days, and from *Stamford* by *Huntington* to *London* in two days more. And the like Stages on their return.

Allowing each Passenger 14ł weight, and all above 3d. a Pound.

Performed By { Benjamin Kingman, Henry Harrison, Walter Baynes,

Also this gives Notice that *Newcastle* Stage Coach, sets out from York, every Monday, and Friday, and from Newcastle every Monday, and Friday.

Rec'd in pt. 05:00: 0 of Mr. Bodingfold for ye p'd for Monday the 3 of June 1706

33. This chimney at the Tadcaster brewery is still a local landmark in the 1970's.

34. William Smith and his two nephews, Henry H. Riley and Frank Riley. William Smith assumed control of the business in 1879.

35. Design for the new Brewery in 1883. "The largest and most complete Brewery in Yorkshire". York Herald.

36. The old advertisement for the Oak Well Brewery at Barnsley.

that Clinch's ghost walks the brewery, for much of the technique and method which he instituted has continued as an efficient routine in this century.

When John Smith died in 1879 he had established Tadcaster without question as a brewing centre and the old days of depression following the collapse of stage coach traffic were forgotten.

It should be mentioned that the death of John Smith caused a curious situation locally which still intrigues visitors to Tadcaster. For next to the brewery which now contains the business of John Smith is the Old Brewery operated by Samuel Smith & Company which is an entirely separate organisation though it is housed in the original brewery premises from which William Smith moved his business toward the end of his life. The reason for this strange juxtaposition lies in John Smith's will. His brother Samuel Smith was a tanner in Leeds and John left his personal estate in equal shares to his brother Samuel and to his bachelor brother William who was with him in his business. His real property of which the Old Brewery formed part was left to the two brothers as tenants in Common for their joint lives; on the death of one to the use of the successor and thereafter entailed generally to the heirs of Samuel Smith. As such items as the barrels and equipment of the brewery came into the category of personal estate, William purchased Samuel's half share. Brother Samuel died in 1880, and William realizing that the business would go to his brother's heirs and not to his sister Sarah Riley's children, who had gone into partnership with him, proceeded to build the new Brewery and before his death transferred the business and the Trade name from the Old Brewery to the new one.

On his death in 1886, the Rileys, as a result of a testamentary request added the name of Smith to their surname. Another result of his death was that the Old Brewery, by that time out of use, reverted to Samuel Smith junior who found himself denied a thriving business which by this time was being carried on next door under the name of and with the goodwill of the founder.

After taking legal advice and finding that as heir to the real property he was not entitled to the trade name, he decided to set up a new business in the Old Brewery which he did with considerable and lasting success. The domestic friction which all this caused was a by-word in Tadcaster in the last century.

"The results of these disagreements", states Mr W. H. D. Riley-Smith, "left a legacy of ill feeling which affected a generation – our Victorian forbears were pretty forthright individuals and were not averse to showing their feelings.

H. H. Riley-Smith died on 19th May, 1911 and Samuel Smith Junr. died on 5th March, 1927.

Since then each of their sons has died and as the years have gone by attitudes, which at one time seem to have been inflexible have softened to friendship and admiration for these are now two successful Companies where only one would have been."

Alfred Barnard compiling his encyclopaedic work on breweries visited the John Smith brewery in 1889 and wrote. . . .

> The history of brewing affords few parallels
> to the rapid and marked progress of Smith's
> brewery during the last ten years; so great is
> the demand for this justly celebrated brew,
> not only in Yorkshire, but in London and all
> parts of England, that from 500 barrels, the
> output has now increased to upwards of 3,000
> barrels per week. This rapid expansion of
> the business is due to the exertions and
> enterprise of the partners, who, for many
> years, have devoted themselves to the study
> of brewing. In their early days, when they
> both served as pupils in the brewery, they
> took their turn at three o'clock in the
> morning with the rest, and lost no opportunity
> of studying the details of the process, hence
> they obtained a practical knowledge of the
> great business which they now possess.

At that time the brewery was employing one hundred people in Tadcaster and there were already sixteen branches opened in various towns. In 1892 the concern became a limited company with a capital of £300,000 and its first directors were the Riley-Smiths who remained on the board until just before the first world war. The present chairman, Mr W. H. Douglas Riley-Smith, started work in the brewery in 1936. He became chairman in 1954.

As the business extended it is interesting to note that it retained one traditional feature, the "Yorkshire Stone Square" system of brewing. This is derived from the fact that the fermenting squares were originally made from stone slabs. The fermenting vessel in which the liquor is contained consists of an enclosed chamber with a manhole in its roof opening into a superimposed chamber of the same area but shallower in depth. The lower chamber is filled with wort and when the fermentation begins the fermenting yeast rises through the manhole into the upper chamber where it collects in a mixture of wort and yeast. About eighteen hours after this frothy head has collected in the upper chamber, the wort is pumped from the lower chamber and discharged into the top chamber. The wort and yeast are then vigorously roused and the wort is run back into the lower vessel leaving the yeast in the top chamber or deck. It was this system which was in use in John Smith's brewery until in recent years the stone squares were replaced by aluminium vessels.

John Smith's beer was first bottled in what was familiarly known as "The Coalyard" in Hodgson's Terrace, Tadcaster, by a local grocer, John William Holiday. It was in about 1907 that the Bottling Store was taken over by John Smith's, and for some years the bottling of naturally matured beer continued there. Bottle washing was done by a hand machine, the dirty bottles being placed in a wheel which slowly revolved through a tank containing caustic solution; then they were brushed out on a revolving brush and finally rinsed with cold water. Crated, they were kept in a warm room ready for the following day. Filling the bottles was rather a slow process when measured by present-day methods, and corking depended upon the hand and foot efforts of the operator. Labelling was similarly done by hand. Beer in those days required some weeks' storage for maturing before sale.

In later years mechanisation of these manual efforts took place, the syphon machine being replaced by a small electrically-driven circular syphon tank. The output from the Bottling Stores in the days of hand filling was somewhere in the region of 500 dozen pints per day, then a considerable achievement.

Like other breweries the expansion of the business at Tadcaster depended upon transportation. On his way from York to Tadcaster Barnard describes how "a stream of drays, numbering thirteen, came in sight and passed us on their way to York and the neighbouring towns". John Smith's brewery horses were indeed famous, not least when they went in procession to York on May Day to compete with others for prizes for the best turned out teams. They were, however, far from being mere show-pieces. The records show that there were dray deliveries as far afield as Pateley Bridge with many stiff gradients to be negotiated in between. Though the coming of railroads had done so much to ruin Tadcaster, they proved to be of great advantage to the expansion of the brewery. A special train of twenty-five trucks pulled out of Tadcaster for Sheffield several days a week. Before the brewery introduced its own mechanised transportation system the railway accounts, covering all classes of traffic through all sources, had reached £48,000 a year.

The first hint of mechanisation was the acquisition of a Fowler steam traction engine reputed to have been first used for hauling stone from the quarries for the building of the new brewery. Later this machine dragged a train of three trailers between the brewery and the railway station – until the road authorities complained of damage and the company directed their attention towards steam lorries which they introduced in 1911. In that year the brewery still owned over 250 horses and pair-horse drays did not go out of service until 1929. At the beginning of the first world war the company was running the first of its petrol driven lorries and these were taken over by the War Department together with some forty of the company horses. During that war, owing no doubt to the shortage of transport, the brewery tried water transportation. They chartered a barge named the "Rosa-Belle" to carry casks of beer from York to Sheffield in time for the Christmas trade. allowing ten days for the trip. She had barely left before the river flooded and the "Rosa-Belle" eventually tied up at her destination some time after the Christmas trade was finished.

At the end of the first world war the company mechanised in a big way purchasing twenty heavy petrol driven lorries. In the 1930s these were superseded by lighter and faster vehicles which were capable of covering the whole of Yorkshire and Lancashire as well as parts of Lincolnshire, Derbyshire and County Durham. These in turn were replaced by the diesels which cover the much greater area now to be serviced.

The Tadcaster Brewery may have had small success with water transport but in the nineteen fifties it had some success with an air-lift. At the end of the second world war John Smith's established a market for Magnet Ale in Belgium. shipping casks from Hull to Antwerp, bottling stores being established in Belgium. The supply was jeopardised by a dock strike in 1950 and John Smith's for a period organised a "Beer-Lift". Two old Halifax bombers were converted to carry seven-ton loads twice daily from an airfield near Tadcaster, the wooden casks being rolled straight from the tails of the diesel lorries into the bomb bays of the Halifaxes. In 1970 the company was still sending to Belgium some 7000 barrels a year – by sea.

During the post-war years the continuing expansion of the business was a major factor in the establishment of Tadcaster as a brewing town. In 1953 John Smith's became a public company. Towards the end of the decade there began a series of mergers and acquisitions which formed the basis of the John Smith's Group which was later to join Courages. By the nineteen-seventies 700 people were being employed by the Tadcaster Brewery and the Company was running a special bus service to take people to and from work. The most important of these new alliances was with the Barnsley Brewery Company which began with a mutual trading agreement in 1957 and was finalised in a merger in 1961.

The Barnsley Brewery, some eighty years old at the time of the merger, possesses a character unlike that of any other element in the Courage Group. The Brewery had been founded and developed largely on the coal mining industry. Situated fairly and squarely in the midst of the capital of the South Yorkshire coalfield, Barnsley's first concern was to quench the prodigious occupational thirst of the pit-workers with Barnsley Bitter and in the boardroom they still say this is "a good ale-supping district". There has always been a strong local feeling for Barnsley Bitter, an emotional loyalty which is as keenly expressed as that for the Barnsley Football Club whose ground adjoins the brewery. That has not meant that the brew was completely localised – fortunately, as it was to turn out. When the merger with Tadcaster took place the Barnsley Company was in possession of over 250 licensed properties already spread over a wide area beyond the confines of the South Yorkshire Coalfield. It was fortunate indeed that the business was not concentrated in Barnsley itself for the pit closures which took place in the 'sixties left not a single colliery working within the town boundary. In the whole area, the rationalisation of the pits brought fewer miners' thirsts to quench but the wider distribution which followed the Tadcaster-Barnsley merger more than compensated for the industrial changes.

Except for its headquarters Beevor Hall, a Georgian mansion built by a bleacher, the Barnsley Brewery, unlike so many other units in the Group had no roots in the eighteenth century. It more than makes up for this by the sense of Victorian and Edwardian tradition which emanates from the place. The brewery was founded about the middle of the nineteenth century by Guy Senior on a site adjoining the Hall. He married the daughter of the owner of Beevor Hall which he later purchased. He prospered. The business was known as Paul and Guy

Senior's Oak Well Brewery and something of the energy and purposefulness of the great Age of Steam is recalled in a magnificent advertisement which was in recent years recovered from an attic. "The original," writes Mr Yorke Crompton in his account of Barnsley, "is several feet long and printed in red and biscuit, blue-grey and green. The Oakwell emblem holds the centre. The advertisement is adorned with drawings from two busts, one of George Stephenson and the other of Joseph Locks. To link the brewery with Britain's other expanding industries, the drawings are reinforced with four vigorous mottoes: 'Coal and Iron England's Greatest Wealth', 'Working Men England's Greatest Strength'. 'No More Bad Trade at Home', 'No More Horse Corn from Abroad'. For good measure, the bottom rim adds: 'Steam Versus Horses – Traction Engines – Home Production – Work for the Million'. The two lower quarters represent a steam traction engine hitched to a brewer's dray. On the left they are standing in front of the Industry Inn, then owned by one George Wilkinson, and still unchanged today in its appearance outwardly; the scene is set, though the picture does not say so, on Barnsley's Baker Street. The other drawing may be described as a high-speed action shot. In it the traction engine is seen puffing down a country road under the direction of a man who usually walked ahead of it to wave a flag. The road is bordered by hedges with curly leaves; behind their cover a policeman crouches like a leopard. For the driver of the traction engine is committing an act of reckless lawlessness – he is driving to the public danger at a speed of over four miles an hour.

"Many times the Seniors were fined for allowing their driver to rush through Yorkshire at this hair-raising pace. Guy Senior welcomed the court cases and the fines, for they proved the enterprise of the brewery in keeping ahead of the times with such rapid deliveries. On the third occasion he told the Bench that he considered these penalties had first-rate advertising value, – indeed, he added. he would gladly pay £10 to Beckett's Hospital for every subsequent conviction."

135

In August 1888 the Senior's business became the Barnsley Brewery Company Ltd with seven directors. all Londoners. Their Memorandum of Agreement covered an exceptionally wide field:– "To carry on business as Brewers. Maltsters, Corn Merchants, Distillers, Hop Merchants, Wine and Spirit Merchants and Importers, Manufacturers of Aerated and Mineral Waters, and other drinks, Licensed Victuallers, Hotel Keepers, Beerhouse Keepers, Restaurant Keepers, Lodging-house Keepers, Farmers, Dairymen, Ice Merchants, Tobacconists, Brick Makers. Bath Keepers, and to buy, sell, manipulate and deal (both wholesale and retail) in commodities of all kinds which can conveniently be dealt in by the Company. . . ." A member of the family Arthur Senior stayed on as brewery manager.

The Company fared badly in the last decade of the nineteenth century. The 1891 Director's Report stated: "The Directors . . . are greatly disappointed that the results of the year's working have not been more satisfactory. The loss in profit is greatly owing to the fact the Malt Kilns have not been used as in former years to their full capacity." In the early part of the present century however things looked up. In 1911 the Chairman reported: "In presenting the 23rd annual report the directors congratulate the shareholders on the continued prosperity of the company. This has been a record year, both for sales and profit in all departments of the business in spite of the high price of hops. and all the inconveniences and drawbacks to which, in these times. brewers have to submit." By that time there was again a Senior on the board and significantly H. E. Umbers a newcomer from Birmingham, who joined the Board in 1908.

After the First World War the business was again in a weakened state and its rehabilitation owed much to a close association between the then Chairman H. J. Wells and Umbers. "The working partnership of the two men, which brought about the renaissance of the company was close." writes Mr Crompton. "For three or four years they actually lived on the premises together as bachelors in one of the

136

cottages. Day and night they talked of the conditions and possibilities at the brewery, to which they dedicated all their efforts. Often they disagreed; sometimes they would argue a point for hours, with warmth as well as with conviction; but basically their common absorbing interest made their relationship harmonious. Their life together at such close quarters was eventually broken up when Wells married and went to live in Victoria Road, Barnsley. But H. E. Umbers, when he also married not long afterwards, continued to live in the cottage at the brewery. And there his son, was born."

Edwin Harry Umbers MBE JP, now President of The Barnsley Brewery Co., born in the brewery cottage, occupied the Chairman's office for many good years, saddened only by the fact that his son who was already prospering in the business died in his prime. During his reign in the post war years a great many of the brewery properties were reconstructed and reconditioned as the mood of the times moved away from austerity toward affluence. These years also saw a phenomenal rise of Working Men's Clubs in the north of England generally but more especially in the South Yorkshire Coalfield where in the Barnsley area alone one hundred and fifty of these clubs were flourishing in the 'seventies. This new social manifestation which originated in the 'thirties and by the 'sixties was so potent in membership, finance and property, is virtually unknown in the south of England. The amenities offered by many of the clubs are lavish, with decoration, with entertainment for all ages from pop to bingo, with games, sometimes with food and always with the mainstay of beer. The freeholds of a certain number of them are owned by the breweries but the great majority are "free". Such a brewery as Barnsley however has very close trading arrangements with many of the free clubs which are made in competition with other breweries.

In 1957 a paragraph in the Yorkshire Post heralded the beginning of a closer association between Barnsley and Tadcaster. "Both companies are in a flourishing condition, and for many years have paid substantial dividends. The Tadcaster company's distribution for the 1st financial year was 15 per cent from an earned surplus of $33\frac{1}{2}$ per cent, while the Barnsley company earned almost 36 per cent and paid 20 per cent." From the trading agreement announced with those figures the companies moved closer and four years later they merged.

That year 1961 the pattern of the John Smith organisation changed dramatically for at the same time as Barnsley, Yates Castle Brewery of Manchester came in under their Chairman J. A. Poë. A few months later they were joined by Warwicks and Richardsons of Newark-on-Trent. This latter concern had older roots than most in the eighteenth century. It was founded on the town wharf at Newark by a brewer named Sketchley who came from Burton-on-Trent in 1766. It afterwards followed a tradition of other breweries in being associated with banking when it was acquired by the Handley family who combined banking with an interest in the Baltic Timber trade. As a result large quantities of ale and porter were shipped to London and the strong ale from the brewery was exported to Archangel in exchange for timber.

Mr Richard Warwick, whose great-grandson is a director at Tadcaster, acquired the business in 1856 and two years later was mayor of Newark. The new Northgate Brewery buildings were erected in 1871 and they seem to have been exceptionally well served by their own fire brigade. The Tourist and Traveller of 1886 referred to this "None of the amateur brigades have approached in completeness those of Messrs Warwicks Brewery brigades. In the fire engine house is an excellent steam Merry-weather kept warm by steam and with its fire ready for immediate ignition 100 lbs of steam may be got up in from five to six minutes and the firemen are summoned by horn during the day and automatic and electrical communication at night."

By 1890 133 people were employed in the business which had a brewing capacity of 100,000 barrels and there were twenty-four branch offices.

Over the years Warwicks and Richardsons, as they became, took in other breweries in Doncaster, Peterborough, Chesterfield and Oundle. These with their licensed houses and hotels merged first with Tadcaster then with the Courage Group which already included another important Newark concern, the business of James Hole.

John Smiths brought into the Group a unique feature - a museum. In a side street off the old turnpike road through Tadcaster is the Ark Museum, a late fifteenth century house owned and run by the Brewery who took it over in 1959 as a building of historic and archaeological value. In 1672 it was licensed as a Dissenters preaching-place and over the years may be said to have fallen from grace to become in turn dwelling house, cobbler's shop, public house, and plumber's workshop. It now houses a curious collection of domestic and industrial by-gones and a growing selection of brewing trade exhibits - open free to the public.

THE SIXTIES

15

The Group was consolidated in the nineteen-sixties as an industrial structure, resting mainly upon the four basic walls of Courages, Barclay Perkins, Simonds and Georges, each founded in the eighteenth century, and the subject of preceding chapters. In the late sixties the Group was in possession of assets of approximately £100m. It was operating five breweries in London, Reading, Bristol, Plymouth and Newark-on-Trent. It owned some 5,000 licensed premises spread over the whole of Southern England, a large part of South Wales and an extensive area of the East Midlands and South Yorkshire.

In the geographical pattern of the Group, features of the past, along with strong local traditions, remained. In many cases, however, their functions had been modified and changed to serve a massive organisation operating in a highly competitive field with up-to-date equipment and a progressive outlook. There was a sensible measure of decentralisation. Courage (Eastern) Limited and Courage (Central) Limited were based in London and Reading respectively to control the Group's activities in South East England and Central Southern England. From Bristol, in the former Georges Brewery by the bridge, Courage (Western) Limited controlled South West England and South Wales. Toward the end of the sixties the firm of James Hole & Co., Ltd., of Newark-on-Trent, had been acquired and the regional headquarters at Newark looked after the Group's interests in the East Midlands and Southern Yorkshire. Anchor Hotels & Taverns Limited, the Group's hotel chain, was managing and progressively modernising a chain of hotels and licensed catering establishments in London and the provinces. The pattern of expansion and nationalisation was continued in the seventies with the acquisition of John Smith's of Tadcaster with widespread interests in the Midlands and the North of England and with the purchase of the important West Country business of Plymouth Breweries.

Social and legislative changes during the sixties increased the significance of wine and spirit wholesaling and of the off-license business operated by the Group.

One of the largest wines and spirits businesses in Britain, Charles Kinloch & Company Limited, joined the Courage Group in 1957 bringing with it a history of wine trading going back 100 years. This firm was stocking some 4,000 lines of wines and spirits, and, apart from its wholesale and retail trade, supplied outlets throughout Britain.

In the off-licence field. the retail trade of Arthur Cooper (Wine Merchant) Limited extended to some 320 off-licences located in most of the major towns in the South of England and South Wales. Off-licence shops were also flourishing under the flag of Saccone & Speed Limited, the famous wine merchants established for more than a century and a quarter, with a special reputation for supplying the Services and the Diplomatic Corps in the world's major capitals. for the Saccone & Speed companies had become part of the Group. Saccone & Speed Limited in Gibraltar operated subsidiary enterprises incorporated in Kenya, Tanzania and Uganda, Malta and North Africa.

Both Barclay Perkins and Simonds had significant export and overseas interests. In the Group, export functions were consolidated through Courage (Export) Limited, which also assumed responsibility for the supervision of overseas interests of which the Blue Nile Brewery Limited, Sudan, and the ownership of approximately one quarter of Simonds-Farsons-Cisk Limited, Malta, were important contributions by Barclay Perkins and Simonds respectively.

Toward the end of the sixties the Group extended its interests as far apart as Scotland and Australia. In Scotland, Melrose-Drover Ltd., whisky blenders, was purchased and in Melbourne,

144

Courage Breweries Ltd., was formed in conjunction with British Tobacco Co., (Australia) Ltd.

In spite of this proliferation in enterprise and in territory, the basic elements – and problems – in the operation of the Group are traditional. Techniques and circumstances change with the times. Yet if the first John Courage came back to meet John Perkins, David Barclay, Blackall Simonds and Philip George to discuss their joint interests as they have merged today, the chances are that they would have no great difficulty in picking up the threads of the business once they had got over the initial surprises and found that it was no longer necessary to calculate by what one horse could do in one day. Their own traditions are alive and not forgotten.

"It is with tinges of regret" writes H. A. Monckton "that we witness the disappearance of the traditional brewer wandering around the brewery with only his sensitive nose, keen palate and a few basic scientific instruments to guide him. Many such brewers armed only with these slender resources have made the product under their control nationally, and even internationally, famous. As we move to a new generation of white-coated technicians bristling with scientific qualifications, guided in their work by panels of flickering lights and working short shifts, we should record our tribute to those practical and hardworking brewers who have gone before with such distinction."

The great brewers of the past would recognise that the four ingredients they acquired and handled with shrewdness and skill – malt, sugar, hops and water – are still as vital as ever in providing a good glass of beer. More than most industries, brewing has retained its close connection with the countryside, for nothing has ever taken the place of the hops and the barley which makes the malt. These mostly come from English fields as they have always done, and the stake of the brewery in agriculture is still significant. Only in the mechanics of growing, harvesting and processing the hops and the barley would the old brewers notice any great change.

The Courage Group in the sixties was still looking to Kent

for supplies of hops. Their stake in the countryside was still considerable, with hopfields covering 200 acres. This agricultural aspect of brewing has also followed the general pattern of mechanisation. After the second World War the special trains which ran out of London carrying hop-pickers to Kent and Sussex to their traditional working holiday gradually ceased to run. By the sixties Londoners in small numbers went "hopping" but no longer specifically to pick, rather to work on various jobs in conjunction with the new machines.

As to the traditional essential grain, the old brewers would look upon the modern maltsters barley no doubt with a specially critical eye and find it greatly to their liking. Constant testing and development of new and better varieties has greatly improved the quality. The turning of barley into malt, a natural process, is now speeded up by mechanisation, but basically the operation remains unchanged.

It fell to the lot of the West Country element in the Courage Group to become the chief provider of malt. The Oakhill Brewery, so long associated with the Hobhouse family, became a mechanised maltings during the sixties. "We were making malt here on the old floor system up to May 1960, and used to produce about 8,000 quarters per year." states H. C. Hobhouse when the new plant was opened. "Under this new system we hope to produce 32,000 quarters a year. We buy the majority of our barleys in Somerset, Devon, Dorset, Hampshire and Wiltshire."

Thus mechanisation has been applied during this century to the practices of the maltster who has gone along with our civilisation for centuries as a benign figure linking the fertile countryside with the thirsty towns. The finished product, the malt in its various qualities for various uses, often still finds its way from the maltings to the brewhouse in the traditional sacks which belong to the old brewery prints. It travels no longer by the rivers and waterways but by road. To take an example, in the biggest malting loft in the Group – that at Horselydown, where the windows face across the river toward the Tower of London as the first John Courage saw it – the sacks of malt stand ready for its various uses, varieties such as Crystal, Burnt Amber and Chocolate Black. As in John Courage's day the brewing process begins with the malt at the top of the building and finishes at the loading docks – no longer waterside wharves – at Thames level. It is a case of everything being changed yet everything remaining the same. The brewers from the past might well be amazed by the size of the operation and impressed by the scale of mechanisation. They would be astonished, perhaps, at the sight of brewery staff in white coats, like doctors, tending instruments and controls in an almost clinical atmosphere. Yet they would recognise an atmosphere of calm almost bordering on tranquillity which, to the casual visitor, is such a marked characteristic of Horselydown. They would soon recognise too that the mechanised processes of the sixties were following a familiar and still unhurried pattern.

The spirit of Dr. Johnson still presides over the site of the former Barclay Perkins Brewery at Southwark where his memory and many of his traditional relics, including his chair, hold places of honour in the Group headquarters. He and the Thrales and their successors would be gratified by the intense activity on the site of their labours, and those of William Shakespeare centuries before. Dr. Johnson who, it will be recalled, stated ". . . we are not here to sell a parcel of boilers and vats . . ." would appreciate the prodigious growth of the enterprise, just as he had prophesied. For the brewery site in the sixties, taking from Shakespeare's theatre the title of The Globe Bottling Store, was established as the most advanced mechanical handling system of any bottling store in the world, with an output capacity of more than a million bottles a day. The beer arrives at the Globe Plant from Horselydown and other Group breweries by road tanker where it is pumped into conditioning or cold storage tanks. Each of these tanks holds 5,760 gallons and together they hold just under 4 million pints of beer. In the warehouse, which has a capacity of more than eight million bottles, overhead cranes stack tham to the height of a three-story building.

147

Apart from the odd cases of empty bottles that are not neatly stacked on the returning lorry, at no time does a man have to lift a crate of full bottles or empty ones. This is automatic to a degree that has never been known in the brewery world, and it has this remarkable end result: a vehicle arriving back at Park Street can have its empties unloaded, a new load put on, and be away again in only three minutes.

This increased speed and precision of mechanisation was a characteristic of the sixties in which the Group was greatly concerned with industrial development. In addition to the developments at The Globe, at Horselydown and at the Oakhill maltings, the Group joined forces with Arthur Guinness Son & Co., Ltd., and Mitchells & Butlers Ltd., to build the Harp Lager Brewery at Alton, the first brewery to be built in Britain since the early thirties. When Harp production began at Alton, lager brewing ceased at Southwark. Also at Alton, but not connected with the Harp enterprise, the Courage Group converted the bottling plant of the old brewery into a canning factory and a bond for export trade. At Bristol the Group extended the brewery site by the bridge and opened an important new bottling store at Avonmouth. In April 1969 Mr. R. H. Courage stated in a speech: ". . . on the work of reshaping ourselves in order that we are ready to cope with the sales forecasts of the seventies, we have spent more than £10m. on our production plants alone."

All that science and technology has given to the brewing industry since the founder members of the Group started their enterprises in the eighteenth century has been made possible by the revolution in transport. The old brewers were tied down by their distribution facilities. Fortunately their successors were always alive to the opportunities offered by transport development. They kept their horses long after many other industries because the horse was so useful for short metropolitan deliveries. But they were quick to make use of steam traction on the roads and to develop an impressive system of distribution by motor vehicle by the middle of this century. By the sixties a fleet

148

of nearly a thousand vehicles was being operated from the breweries, bottling stores and depots spread over the Group's trading area. They range from 24-ton tankers to small delivery vans. More than 12,000 deliveries were being made each week, 4,000 of them in the London area alone. Distribution was extensively method-studied and large sums were spent on specialised articulated vehicles and on the long distance bulk transport fleet to meet the rapidly growing bulk export trade with Europe and to take advantage of the permission to run larger vehicles on British roads.

It was the localised nature of distribution which originally led to the acquisition by the brewer, often also a banker, of retail outlets within the area in which his transport allowed him to operate. This system of tied houses became even more of a necessity during the latter part of the nineteenth century and afterwards, when the law demanded more exacting conditions in pubs and hotels. Alterations and enlargements were often too onerous for the local inn-keeper with limited capital, faced also with increasing rates and overheads and the steady rise in property prices. So the brewers, apart from the kind they acquired for their own industrial plant and their agricultural needs, bought property on a scale which of course increased as transportation enabled them to spread their territories, and mergers further extended the territorial scope. "The tremendous responsibility for property in the form of licensed houses is not always realised," recently noted the editor of the Brewer's Guild Journal; "Many skills are required in its administration and a vast amount of money has been and still is spent on mainten-ance and improvement of property."

Writing in the mid-sixties in the National Provincial Bank Review, Mr. R. H. Courage explained the current operation of the tied house system as it applied to brewing in general. "While admittedly at the outset it proved far from satisfactory in operation, it has by evolution become the highly efficient system for which there is no exact parallel in any other industry. It enables the brewer to plan production and, as the majority of his outlets are reasonably concentrated, he is in a position also to plan the maintenance, repair and general administration of the houses to the best advantage. He can ensure a regular flow of orders and regulate production accordingly. He is able to zone his deliveries and, indeed. throughout most of his operations to work to fine limits with a maximum of economy.

"It would not be very wide of the mark to say that the ultimate test of efficiency in any industry must be the value the customer receives for his money. By this standard the tied house system is one of the most efficient marketing methods of the present day."

The application of this line of thought specifically to the activities of the Courage Group led to the formation of the Horselydown Property Investment Company which operates in partnership with leading companies in property development and on its own account throughout the territory in which the Group is interested. In common with the other great brewery concerns, the Courage Group was involved throughout the sixties in a continuous programme of modification and improvement involving property development.

More than at any other time during the present century, the sixties showed changes in public taste and attitude toward refreshment (both food and drink) and entertainment.

The brewers, more than most industrialists, have to be aware of such social changes and to keep abreast of them in a highly competitive situation. Fortunately tradition has helped. Throughout the long history of family brewing, some of which is recorded in the preceding pages, the fact emerges that the brewer always had to be on the alert for changes in public taste and need. This was shown in the switchover to porter when it was in great demand, to the increase in the production of beer in bottles, to the various emergency measures taken in two wars. To be sufficiently flexible in operation and sensitive to the market is indeed a tradition without cobwebs to be cherished.

The social conditions of the sixties effected a dramatic rise in the standards of living and entertainment which had to be reflected in the amenities of the public houses if these were to survive and flourish in an atmosphere of intensified competition. The impact of almost universal coverage of the British Isles by television – and in the sixties it became unusual for a family not to possess a television set – created a new sophistication in public taste and a new focus on home life. The 'local' found itself in competition with the family 'telly'. Consequently the 'local' had to brighten itself up and sometimes to provide some television facilities. Its new look also had to appeal to the more sophisticated appetites which television was producing. The effort was made and it succeeded. In spite of the prophets of doom, the 'locals' held their place in the Television Age. The pattern of drinking changed; there was more consumption in the home. For the Courage Group this change was well served by the chain of Arthur Cooper and Saccone & Speed off-licences. But a mass audience for television did not seriously diminish the affection of the public for the 'local'. The pub remained a social amenity but only through having moved with the times.

The sixties was also a period of unprecedented foreign travel for people in every income group. This again increased the sophistication of public taste for such drinks as lager and wine, for entertainment and for decorative environment. So more and more facilities for good food were needed and provided. Not only in the Anchor Hotels and Taverns, but in public houses throughout their territory the Courage Group – like the other big brewers – offered their customers good food on a scale unknown before. The emphasis on food went with a new social attitude toward drinking, and the overall effort made by the brewing industry was described as a "package-deal" by Lord Boyd, Chairman of The Brewer's Society writing in The Financial Times in the mid-sixties: "Investing nearly £1,000m. in licensed properties, brewers have replaced the comfortless drinking shops of the last century with attractive and well-furnished 'locals', selling food as well as drink and providing facilities for club meetings, receptions and other social activities. It is the sort of positive effort which probably has far more effect on national sobriety in the long run than many of the inhibitions imposed by law.

"This special contribution by the trade has been well described as a 'package-deal'. The 'pint in a pub' is not a commodity in itself but part of the deal. Not more than 15 per cent of customers choose their public house primarily for the beer. if a Hulton survey made some years ago is generally applicable."

Another aspect of the changing scene in the sixties as it affected the Courage Group was in advertising. The emergence of the television networks provided new platforms for products to be advertised on a massive scale. When the brewer was operating in small units advertising was localised and on a small scale. The formation of the Courage Group and its association with Harp Lager, the brewing industry's most notable success story of the period, enabled the enterprise to benefit from national and regional advertising in all media, including television.

Finally, the association with lager products has been significant in the export trade. Each of the constituent members of the Courage Group has a history of overseas trading going back to its earliest days – not least to the Court of Catherine the Great. These activities were integrated by the formation of Courage (Export) Limited which markets beer, wines and spirits all over the world in bulk, bottle and can, and Courage products are to be found on most of the world's shipping lanes.

In reviewing the state of health of the Group during the sixties, employing some 15,000 people and producing something like 75 million gallons of beer yearly, it is not possible to explore all the complexities of an intricate industrial organisation which still remains closely related to agriculture. It can only be noted that tradition continues to play a dynamic part, although it must be skilfully blended with a day to day flexibility and an adventurous attitude toward the techniques of the times. These qualities were all shared in some measure by John Courage and Philip George, by Blackall Simonds, by Barclay and Perkins and by John Smith, the founders.